CRACE
to Run the Race

JOURNEYS IN THE REALMS OF HEAVEN

by

Valerie Henderson

GRACE
to Run the Race

Journeys in the Realms of Heaven

By

Valerie Henderson

PO Box 2132

Keller, Texas 76244

USA

Table of Contents

Acknowledgements

I want to first thank the Holy Spirit for guiding me through Heaven's realm to share with others about God's grace to run the race. I appreciate my awesome husband John for encouraging me to keep writing and moving forward on this book.

I especially want to acknowledge David and Jaye Arsement, Jim Ryder, Brandy Anderson, Debra Tillery, Becky Dobyns and Morris Graves, Jr. who have supported me through impeccable prayer and words of encouragement. Special thanks to Becky Dobyns for editing this book for me as well. I am sincerely grateful for Ron Horner's helpful insight to bring the book to final completion for publishing. Darian Horner for her creativity in designing the front and back cover. Thank you all.

Foreword

Hunger is the word that best describes what I have seen from Valerie in the few years I have known her. From the first time I met her in Arlington, Texas, at a conference I was conducting until the present day she has had an insatiable desire for the presence of God and the realms of Heaven. The first thing I had the attendees do at that conference was to take a step into the realms of Heaven. Valerie did and she shares that encounter in Chapter 10. (I won't spoil it for you!)

Then, a few months later she came to another conference I held in North Carolina and she had more encounters with Heaven and the things of Heaven (Chapters 13 & 14). However, Valerie did not limit her encounters to special events. It has become for her a way of life.

We learned years ago that we need not limit our encounters with Heaven until after we have passed from this earth. We are spirit beings and need to live acutely aware of Heaven and its reality. After all, the spiritual realm is the reality while the earth is simply the vapor (James 4:14).

We are encouraged by the words of the Apostle Paul to seek the things that are above (in Heaven) and not the things of the earth. (Colossians 3:1). Valerie has learned to do this as you will discover in this wonderful, encouraging book. Heaven is very real to her and can be just as real to you.

Her stories are at times raw but always very real. Her life has witnessed horrific tragedies but as she describes, she was never alone. Jesus was always nearby. Whether on a mountaintop or the deepest valley Valerie has learned to continue the journey and let Heaven be her comfort.

What I taught at those conferences about accessing the realms of Heaven are quite simple. If you are a believer in Jesus, then you are a citizen of Heaven; therefore, we have rights of access to Heaven and we do not have to die physically to experience Heaven. Simply by faith take a step into the realms of Heaven. I often have the audience conduct a prophetic act of standing, closing their eyes, focus on Jesus and make a simple statement. "Father, by faith I take a step into the realms of Heaven." As they say these words, I encourage them to simply take a step forward into Heaven and notice what they see, hear, or sense. Typically, they can quickly note the peacefulness of the atmosphere and the beauty of Heaven. It is just that simple. I invite you as you read of her encounters, pause, and allow them to become your own. She beautifully describes the wonders of Heaven so picture yourself alongside Valerie as she shares her many journeys in the realms of Heaven.

The fact is, you and I belong in Heaven. Our purpose here on the earth is to encourage as many others as possible to join us in our journey to Heaven. That is what Valerie is doing with the words of this book and may Heaven become as real to you as it is to her. Join her; it is quite an adventure!

Dr. Ron M. Horner
LifeSpring International Ministries
CourtsOfHeaven.net

Preface

When the Lord told me years ago that He would perform "heart surgery" on me after the tragedy that befell my family, I never could have imagined the beautiful journey in the Spirit that awaited me.

The Holy Spirit so sweetly and gently guided me in healing my heart. He helped me feel the sweet love of my Heavenly Father as He filled the wounds left by my earthly father. I'm just an ordinary person, yet He lets me see into the Heavenly realm with great frequency, sometimes when I'm just preparing for work, going about my day, or even stopped at a red light.

It is my joy to share these moments with you. As you read, I invite you to let Him heal your own heart and sweep you up in the great adventure He has for you. I believe He desires these Heavenly visions for everyone, that He wants to reveal His secrets to us even more than we want to seek them.

As you read these words, I bless you with the heart of a child. I bless you with the sweetness and humility of Christ. Whatever you have been through in your past, whether tragedy or loss you have witnessed, I bless you with a restored innocence that only Jesus can give.

I pray that as you read these visions the Lord has blessed me with, you are swept up into the Heavenly places. I pray that there are many moments you need to lay the book aside so that you can soak in the presence of the Lord for yourself, bask in His goodness, and see the treasures He has laid up for you in Heaven.

No matter who you are or where you have been, He has a mansion prepared just for you in Heaven. All who confess with their mouth that Jesus is Lord and simply believe in their hearts that God raised Him from the dead will be saved, no matter who you are, where you have been, or what you have done.

Not only does He want each of us with Him in Heaven, but He wants all of us to live in Heaven on earth. When your time here on earth is done, I pray that you get to walk into places in Heaven that are already familiar to you because you visited them on earth. Even in your most anxious moments, when you feel stressed out, worn, and weary, you can lock eyes with Jesus and be in the Throne Room in an instant.

May you know, as you read these precious visions of Heaven on the pages that follow, how much the Lord delights in you, how much He sings over you, how many good plans He has for you.

He is truly El Roi — the God Who Sees — and He has seen all your hardships and suffering. He will waste none of it, dear one. Only humble yourself and come to Him as a little child, handing Him your grief, anger, pain, and all the things you do not understand. Let Him restore your soul with visions of Heaven and the beautiful things He has prepared for you.

Chapter 1

Abide in Me

I am standing at the window of my future, staring out and wondering if you will come abide with me. My heart is breaking tonight as I wait for you. My mother has been murdered, my dad was the murderer, and now he is dead by suicide. Left an orphan, I see it all in my thoughts as if it were yesterday when my world came crashing down in one swift swipe. Like a farmer out in his field winnowing with his sharp tool and cutting the wheat down for harvest, in one swift decision my earthly father changed the course of my future.

My thoughts rush to the Bible verse that says, "The thief comes only to steal and kill and destroy" (John 10:10). Why, Lord, must this unspeakably horrible and sad experience happen to me and my family? What did we do to deserve such a tragic circumstance? Oh Father, help me walk this road that You have chosen for me, a narrow path that will lead to You and Your righteousness.

I open the window of my future, lean out, take a deep breath, and inhale Your breath of life deep within my soul. As I exhale, I feel Your strength rise within me, Heavenly Father. Strength I cannot get anywhere else.

Feeling Your presence near me now, I stick my head back in the quiet room, rush to the door, grab the handle, and open it. I run out through a garden to a gate. I open it and see the gatekeeper standing there, who says, "I will abide in you, and you in Me."

I fall in His arms weeping. "Jesus, Jesus, thank You for coming to abide with me and for rescuing me. You have taken my burdens and given me Your yoke that is light. Oh, Heavenly Father, You have not left me alone because of Your loving kindness toward me. I know You will be with me even unto my journey's end and until I walk into Your everlasting arms for all eternity."

Father, Your Son said that many are called, but few are chosen. I tell You today that no matter my circumstance, I will choose You, Father, and Your Son, Jesus the Messiah. Today I let You transform my heart, circumcising it and putting away the sin in me. All the fear, hate, bitterness, and selfishness — I lay it all down at the cross.

Jesus takes me by the hand, gently leads me out of the garden, and rushes me past a storm in the distance. He leads me to a hospital, and we go in. Suddenly, we are standing in a prep room. I look up and see Jesus, the Great Physician, with His scrub clothes on. I walk into the operating room, see a woman lying on the table, and realize she is one of my older sisters.

I ask Jesus, "What kind of surgery is she going to have?" He replies, "Heart surgery."

I turn to look at Him and ask, "Will I have heart surgery too?" Jesus says, "Yes, but not here. Your surgery will take place at another hospital." I look into His eyes and they pierce my soul. His Spirit awakens me, and I know what He speaks will one day come to pass.

I leave the hospital and walk back into the world. Though much strife will still come my way, now I know I will be equipped to withstand the fiery darts of the enemy. "The future of your destiny will be glorious," says the Lord.

I smile as I see the gatekeeper holding the gate open for my return home. He calls to me as I walk toward the narrow path ahead and says, "I give my angels charge over you." Tears come to my eyes. As I wipe the tears from my cheeks, I look up and see His angels guiding me safely along the narrow path.

I look back one more time to Jesus and ask, "When will I return home?" He gently replies, "I go to prepare a place for you. In my Father's house there are many mansions." I smile back at Him and tell Him, "I can't wait to see it, no matter where my journey is about to take me." I feel so much assurance in His voice, and it gives me new hope for the long journey ahead of me. I know His everlasting love for me will now carry me far beyond my expectations. Trusting in Him, I begin my journey down the narrow path.

Come what may, I tell myself, I shall not lean unto my own understanding, but His.

Chapter 2

On Earth as It Is in Heaven

I look forward to tomorrow as I walk down the narrow path. With assurance, I move forward. Though I do not know what may lie ahead, I know God holds my past and my future. My soul sings, "Thy will be done on earth as it is in Heaven." My spirit is now walking in tune with His Holy Spirit.

My heart and soul skip to the tunes of the Heavenly Father, and my soul knows well that the joy of the Lord is my strength. "Oh hallelujah," sings my soul, "Oh hallelujah, blessed be the name of the Lord. Set apart is His name."

Jesus said we are not of this world, and surely my soul rejoices upon hearing such news. He told us that the world would hate us, but God's Word will sustain us. God gave us the Word that we may know the Truth that sets us free from the world and its hate toward those who believe in Him. "I believe, I believe," says my soul to the Heavenly Father, who is and is to come.

On the narrow path, the Father has given us the power to cast out demons, break generational curses, and lay hands on the sick and the blind so that they all are healed. We pray for the dead, and they rise and live. The anointing of the Holy Spirit He has given freely to those who have chosen to take up their cross and follow Him daily. We live and speak His Word, His wisdom, with every breath we take.

Jesus said of those who are His that He would abide in them. Let my soul say, "He will abide in me, and I will abide in Him." Let us live Heaven here on earth. We do not have to wait until we die to experience Heaven; we can live it on earth now. The experience of Heaven is in us now. Our Father who is in Heaven, let it be done on earth as it is in Heaven.

His righteousness reigns. His love the world does not know, but to those who know Jesus, He has declared to us God's love and His name. The love with which God loved His Son is the same love with which He loves us. "For God so loved the world, that He gave His only begotten Son, that whosoever believeth in Him should not perish, but have everlasting life."

John 3:16 means Heaven is here for us today, right now. Not next week or next year. But right now, we can live Heaven on earth. No need to die first to enjoy the benefits of Heaven. Jesus came to give us life and give it more abundantly. We have liberty in the Lord, for greater is He in me than he who is in the world. The joy of the

Lord is my strength. Let my soul be on fire, a flame that will never go out.

Oh, praise God, Heaven lives in me today. I will experience Heaven in me today, not tomorrow.

Chapter 3

The Vinedresser

Along my journey, I come to rest under the shade of a tree. Its branches are strong and spread out with many leaves. I sit and enjoy the cool of the shade and wipe the sweat from my brows.

I look across the way and see a beautiful vineyard of many grapevines. As I glance over the vineyard, I can hear the words of Jesus:

"I am the true vine, and My Father is the vinedresser. [2] Every branch in Me that does not bear fruit He takes away; and every branch that bears fruit He prunes, that it may bear more fruit. [3] You are already clean because of the word which I have spoken to you. [4] Abide in Me, and I in you. As the branch cannot bear fruit of itself, unless it abides in the vine, neither can you, unless you abide in Me. [5] "I am the vine, you are the branches. He who abides in Me, and I in

him, bears much fruit; for without Me you can do nothing.
(John 15:1-5)

With the reminder of this word, I quickly gain my strength to continue my journey toward my destiny. I stand up, dust the dirt off my clothes, and take off running the good race.

Lord, let me bear fruit today. Let Your Word so live in me that others will know that you abide in me, and I in You. Jesus, You said:

As the Father loved Me, I also have loved you; abide in My love. 10 If you keep My commandments, you will abide in My love, just as I have kept My Father's commandments and abide in His love.

11 These things I have spoken to you, that My joy may remain in you, and that your joy may be full. 12 This is My commandment, that you love one another as I have loved you. 13 Greater love has no one than this, than to lay down one's life for his friends. 14 You are My friends if you do whatever I command you. 15 No longer do I call you servants, for a servant does not know what his master is doing; but I have called you friends, for all things that I heard from My Father I have made known to you. 16 You did not choose Me, but I chose you and appointed you that you should go and bear fruit, and that your fruit should remain, that whatever you ask the Father in My name He may give you. 17 These things I command you, that you love one another. (John 15:9-17)

Oh, Heavenly Father, as I run the good race, I inhale and exhale to fill every part of my being with Your breath of life. Your breath gives my soul and spirit the strength and endurance they need to fulfill Your commandments of love toward others. You are the vinedresser and I the branch. You have pruned my branch in its due season so that I may produce fruit from the vine that is everlasting and reflects the Messiah, Your Son.

Chapter 4

Like Deer's Feet

I am staring out into the night sky, my heart broken over my sister's death. She was eight years older than me.

The stars in the sky seem different tonight. It seems they have lost their luster of brilliant shine. Tears are flowing from my eyes so heavily that I can barely see them through the blur. Lord, where are You tonight? I need You here holding onto me. I cannot stop thinking about my sister. I know that, in Your goodness and kindness, You will show up for me.

I turn to walk back into the house, the loneliness in my heart more than can bear at this moment. As I enter the door of my house, I feel a tug at my heart and hear Jesus saying, "Here I am." I turn around, reach out, and take His hand. The tender look on His face tells me He is going to carry this heavy burden for me. Jesus comes to heal the brokenhearted, and this night He sits with me in my dark bedroom as I rock in my chair in the corner of the room. I whisper into the darkness, "Father, I lean into you tonight."

Jesus' love tonight is like a flower in full bloom with the tender petals of a rose. Yet my heart wants to be in a far, desolate place away from it all so that I can weep for my sister. Jesus speaks to me and reminds me of what he told the apostles: "Come aside by yourselves to a desert place and rest a while."

This evening, I sit for many hours by myself; it is a time to inhale and exhale once again, be still, and know that God is the caregiver of the brokenhearted. The God of all the universe gives me everything I need tonight to continue my journey along the narrow path of life.

As I stand up from my glider chair, I wipe the tears from my eyes and thank Jesus for sitting with me in the dark. He stands up, walks toward me, and hands me a beautiful blue bottle full of clear liquid with a cork in the top of it. I gaze down at the bottle and read the label. It reads, "All the tears you have cried for your sister."

I look up at Jesus. He says, "These are your tears the Father collected, and He knows there will be many more before tomorrow is here." I lean into His chest and cry as He softly strokes my head.

As I begin to gain strength from His nearness, Jesus transports me to a rocky trail alongside a hill. A storm in the distance rolls in, and it begins to rain down on me. The raindrops hit me in the face so hard that I can barely see to make my way down the rocky path. I cry, "Jesus, help me! I'm scared." The trail is ending, and for a moment I think I might fall off the side of the hill. Then the Holy Spirit whispers to my heart, "The Lord God is your strength; He will make your feet like deer's feet. He will make you walk on high hills, and your path will not be slippery."

That night, the Lord renewed my strength. I mounted up on eagles' wings and was able to enter the good race ahead of me and not grow weary.

Chapter 5

Before I Formed You

In my quiet time at my desk, as I read the words from the Bible, I pause for a moment and stare into the air.

In a vision, I hear the voice of my mother telling my dad she is pregnant again. Knowing this will be their eleventh child, she asks him how he feels. He says, "We will manage, just like we have with all our other children." She rests her hand on her stomach. In her heart, she is hoping they will be able to afford this child. Another mouth to feed, clothe, and house. As Dad leaves the room, Mother sits and ponders about the new life that is growing inside of her.

I see Jesus kneel and tenderly touch her stomach. He looks upon my mother with great compassion. He knows her worries and speaks into the Heavenly realm that Mother cannot see or hear. Yet on that day, the words he speaks ring out through all of Heaven: "Before I formed her in the womb, I knew her; Before she was born, I sanctified her. I ordained your daughter a prophet to the nations."

"Father," I declare, "You predestined and designed me. I am your child, and you do have a calling on my life."

I was born on a Saturday, which is God's Sabbath, a day of rest. It was also Valentine's Day — the sweetest day of the year, a day when people all over the world celebrate love for one another. I see now that His banner over me is love, and that banner was flying high in God's Kingdom that day.

Oh Lord, let me spread that banner of love to the entire world, just as You have shown it to me. Your eyes saw my substance, being yet unformed, and in Your book, they are all written, the days fashioned for me. How precious are your thoughts to me, O God! How great is the sum of them! If I should count them, they would be more in number than the sand.

O my soul, inhale and exhale the breath of God, and rejoice in the Lord. His banner over you is love. God knew you when he formed you in the secret places. Dance, soul, dance before the Lord, for He is your keeper. The Lord says, "For I am with you to deliver you. Tell me today what your need is, and I will send you My bountiful treasures from afar. I will fix your broken vessel so that the living waters of Heaven can flow through your belly." In the fear of the Lord I find His righteousness of love. His love reigns over all the peoples of the earth.

As I sit in my room, I see deeper into the vision. My mother is holding me, her new baby daughter, in a pillow, for I was born so tiny. She cuddles me in the pillow, feeding me my nighttime bottle as she rocks me to sleep, praying over me that my tiny body will grow strong and not weak. Jesus walks into the room and quietly touches my tiny body so that it will grow strong, and then He says, "This day I have not left her an orphan. I send my Holy Spirit to comfort her." He knows what my future will bring.

The future is here and now, and the good race is still on. It is shouting out God's love and plan for all. The Word of God says, "In the fear of the Lord there is a strong confidence. And His children will have a place of refuge. The fear of the Lord is a fountain of life, to turn one away from the snares of death" (Proverbs 14:26-27). Let my heart be merry that "the name of the Lord is a strong tower; the righteous run to it and are safe" (Proverbs 18:10).

I run to You, Lord, today. You encompass my steps, and they are preset by you. I hear the Spirit of the Lord echo, "Even when you have faith, hope, and love, the greatest of these three will always be love." Thank you, Heavenly Father. I can see clearly now that my path of destiny is glorious because of Your love for me, for love covers a multitude of sins.

Chapter 6

In Spirit & In Truth

As I take my morning walk in the Heavenly realm of God, I come upon a beautiful bench made of stone. It has been thoughtfully placed so that one can sit and enjoy the peaceful river that runs alongside the banks.

As I walk up closer to the bench, I see Jesus sitting there. I feel like Esther approaching the king, hoping He will extend his welcome to me by holding out his scepter, giving me permission to come to him.

Jesus stands up, greets me, extends His hand, and smiles. I know that the invitation has been given. My heart leaps like a gazelle jumping in splendor across the grass. Jesus speaks these words to me: "I have been waiting for you. I want to teach you about true worship in spirit and truth." I reply, "I am ready."

I turn toward the river. It becomes a solid floor, and I see Heavenly worshipers appear on the floor of Heaven. They bow in humility, then stand up and sing, "Holy, holy, holy is the Lord God Almighty." The music of Heaven begins to play, and the worshipers begin to dance in one accord, worshiping the King of kings and Lord of lords. The Spirit of God descends among them like a dove.

His Holy Spirit moves gracefully upon them. Like a ballerina in her finest moment, the dancers flow across the floor, and the Spirit of the Lord invites me into the midst of them to dance and worship. They teach me that the humility in our hearts is what moves the Holy Spirit to greater depths of worship. It brings Heaven down on earth with every sincere move and thought within our soul. As I dance and worship across the floors of Heaven, my soul sings out with all the worshipers, "Great is the Lord, and greatly to be praised in the city of our God."

As I continue to worship, I see a vision of Jesus walking across the water to the disciples in the boat amid the storm, calming the raging waters into a solidified, peaceful floor. He loves to change our troubled waters into joyful dance floors. When He calmed the storm, Jesus was teaching that faith is the substance of things hoped for (Hebrews 11:1) and will move the Spirit of God into action, making even a river into a solid substance for His true worshipers.

As my spirit moves across Heaven's floor, I tell my soul to inhale and exhale the breath of God my Creator, feeling and absorbing every moment in this place of worship with the Lord. "Hallelujah! Bless the Lord," whispers my soul. As the deer pants for the water, so pants my soul for You, O God. My soul thirsts for God as I lift my hands in praise, singing praises to our God.

As I dance with the true worshipers, Jesus comes and stands amid Heaven's floor, watching me. I find myself lost in the ecstasy of His everlasting love for me. I feel no shame as my spirit moves in sync with His Spirit. As Jesus speaks, I see His words dance around me in sweet softness, and He says, "The hour is coming, and now is, when the true worshipers will worship the Father in spirit and truth; for the Father is seeking such to worship Him. God is spirit, and those who worship Him must worship in spirit and truth" (John 4:23-24).

I respond, "Father, let all those rejoice who put their trust in You; let them ever shout for joy, because You defend them; let those also who love Your name be joyful in You. For You, O Lord, will bless the righteous; with favor You will surround him as with a shield" (Psalm 5:11-12). He tells me, "When you move into a place of true worship before the Lord, you will know it within. The Holy Spirit will guide you and teach you all you need to know because of your humility. The greater humility in your heart, the greater depth of worship you will experience with all of Heaven and its true worshipers."

"Show me Your ways, O Lord; teach me Your paths. Lead me in Your truth and teach me, for You are the God of my salvation; on You I wait all the day" (Psalm 25:4-5) "The humble He guides in justice, and the humble He teaches His ways. All paths of the Lord are mercy and truth, to those who sincerely seek His face and ask to be pardoned from all their iniquity" (Psalm 25:9-10). The Lord is near to all who call upon him in truth.

Dance, soul, dance, and worship the Lord in spirit and truth. Blessed are the pure in heart, for they shall see God.

Chapter 7

The Lord's House

As the Spirit of the Lord moves among the true worshipers, I feel the Father's holy presence move across the floor of Heaven as angels appear and sing, "Holy, holy, holy is the Highest God. The Alpha and Omega, the Beginning and the End." A holy fire is released upon all the true worshipers as one by one they begin to prophesy and speak in Heavenly tongues, lifting the God of all the earth.

Each true worshiper steps forward, bows, and leaves Heaven's floor with a heart of thanksgiving, each one receiving their commission to go forth and preach the good news of the Ancient of Days. I am the last to leave Heaven's floor, and I, too, bow before Jesus the Messiah. As I stand up, an angel steps forward and hands me a scroll, which I carefully unroll.

It reads, "The Lord's house shall be established on the top of the mountains, and it shall be exalted above the hills; and all nations shall flow to it. Many people shall come and say, come and let us go up to the mountain of the Lord, to the house of the God of Jacob; He will teach us His ways, and we shall walk in His paths" (Isaiah 2:2). Then the angel takes the scroll from me and sends it out with the ministering angels to establish the word of the Lord throughout all the earth.

As I stand before the Lord on Heaven's floor, I hear the voice of Isaiah saying, "O house of Jacob, come and let us walk in the light of the Lord" (Isaiah 2:5). The Spirit of the Lord lets me understand that though this word was spoken and given to Isaiah for the house of Jacob in the ancient days, it is still a timely prophecy in this day and age for those who have ears to hear and eyes to see what God is doing in the Heavenly realms, preparing those whom he has called to come to the mountain of God.

Our spirit within us longs for the mountaintops because God lives there. Our soul well knows where God's house resides, and that is why Moses' spirit is still calling out to us from the pages of the Bible, "Go to the mountaintop to meet with God."

Only when we have gone to the house of the Lord on top of the mountain will we be able to receive the holy fire of the Lord. This fire transforms our fleshly being so that we can understand how God cares about the appearance of our hearts before Him, just as He did with Moses. Meeting with God changes how we see the world and its views. It allows us to see what Moses saw: man, and God in relationship with one another — not striving against each other, but one in spirit, living in unity, for we who are in Christ are a new creation.

Like Moses going to the mountaintop to meet with God, our inner spirits are transformed by every word He speaks. Moses knew he must go to the mountain to meet with God to continue to lead the Israelites into the Promised Land; it was not an option.

Let us not wander in the desert for 40 years when we have been given the opportunity to finish our journey across the desert at His invitation — to come to His house on the mountain, visit with Him, and receive instructions so we can know the path to take to His promises. When we listen to His voice, our path that lies before us will not be slippery but rather filled with His benefits that lead us to His everlasting ways.

How will you know what spoken word the Lord has for you and others if you do not make the journey to the top of the mountain? We must find our own spiritual mountains with God within our hearts. Only then can we advance with Him to the next level to strategically do the work He has called us to do as He gives us the power and ability to stop our unseen enemies in their tracks.

Jesus said, "My house shall be called a house of prayer." Come, let us go to the house of the Lord, confess our sins one to another, and pray for one another so the quenching fire of the Holy Spirit can set us free from all pride our hearts hold deep within us. Let us go up to the Lord's house. Then each of us can say, "It is well with my soul."

Heavenly Father, thank you for establishing Your presence in all the earth, so that the world will know You are the God who never slumbers and who watches over His people day and night. Lord, let me be faithful with Your Word, sharing it freely to those who are lost and without You.

O Lord transform our hearts today to live a righteous life, so that the world will know we have been to the mountaintop to learn Your ways. Create a clean heart in me, O God, and renew a right spirit within me. Guide me into Your everlasting ways. Let Your light shine in me so that others will know Your love, a love that gives mercy and forgiveness to all who seek You. Seek the Lord while He may be found. Come, let us go to the house of the Lord, who reigns on high forevermore.

I step with Jesus back onto the riverbank, and the river begins to flow softly, with a quietness that speaks through its shimmering, peaceful waters. Even the river knows it is in the presence of the Lord. Jesus and I walk for a while along the path of the bank. With His arm around me, we continue in sweet silence. My spirit speaks:

O LORD, You have searched me and known me. ² You know my sitting down and my rising up; You understand my thought afar off. ³ You comprehend my path and my lying down and are acquainted with all my ways. ⁴ For there is not a word on my tongue, but behold, O LORD, You know it altogether. (Psalm 139:1-4)

Jesus and I stop walking for a moment. He gently turns me around to face Him and hugs me. I feel His love burst through me like a newborn star in the heavens. I press my entire being into His chest, not wanting to let go of this moment with my Savior. I lift my head and look up at Him. He thanks me for coming to visit and then sends me on to complete my journey along the path with the Holy Spirit. I look back to Jesus, wanting to run back and stay with Him a while longer, but I know I must continue to run the good race to which He has called me. "Sing," I tell my spirit, "sing, for you have been to the house of the Lord."

Chapter 8

The Sparrow

Along the riverbank, I follow a trail that leads deep into a forest. A sparrow follows me. As I advance into Heaven's forest, the sparrow flies ahead of me and waits on a branch up in the trees as I leave the path of the river behind.

I continue the trail through the forest for a while, with no sense of time. I'm not here to count the miles.

The little sparrow seems to enjoy me coming to visit his home. The Lord's presence abides in every living thing in the forest. Even the rocks cry out with praise, and the trees clap their hands unto to the Most High God of Heaven. I can feel the joy of the Lord in all His creation throughout the forest.

As I feel God's presence coursing through this place, I am reminded of my visit to the mountain of God before visiting here. I can hear Moses' voice speak these words: "Lord, You have been our dwelling place in all generations. Before the mountains were brought forth, or ever You had formed the earth and the world, even from everlasting to everlasting, You are God" (Psalm 90:1-2). I quietly think on those words as I walk slowly on the trail, looking in awe at the splendor of the beauty of the forest.

In the distance I hear a waterfall, and I walk the trail toward the sound of the water flowing over the edges of a cliff. I come to rest on the green grass beside the pool of water that it gathers into. Glancing across the water, I realize that in Heaven's forest, all creatures small and large live in unison with one another. I see the lion lying with the lamb and bow my head in humility before our Creator, thanking Him for this opportunity to see firsthand how all creation is to abide in Him.

My soul tells me that in this forest, the Lord is turning my ashes into beauty. I am grateful for everything the Lord is revealing to me about my life while I sit and rest by the pool of water. The pleasant smell of the forest refreshes my spiritual senses, and I am carried away by the thought of how precious it is to know the rose of Sharon, Jesus our Messiah.

I had forgotten about the little sparrow that had watched my every step into the forest. With joy, I'm reminded of his presence as he flies to me, sits upon my lap, and allows me to gently stroke his head. His feathers are so soft, and the glitter of Heaven shines from his coat of feathers. Once again, I am in awe that in God's dwelling place all creation lives in unity with one another. I know that one day, earth will rest from the toll of sin mankind has taken upon it.

The earth is the Lord's; it is His footstool. All creation cries out for God to come and give us rest from man's self-proclaimed righteousness. In God's Kingdom, the words from all the prophets that have gone before us ring out through all of Heaven. If we will be still and know He is God, we will hear the prophecies of the Ancient of Days continue to call out to us, prompting us to seek the Lord while He may be found. There is a day coming when mankind will live in unity with one another and turn their weapons into plows and shovels, for God will reign on His holy mountain in Jerusalem once again.

Rejoice in the Lord, O you righteous! For praise from the upright is beautiful. I sing a new song to Lord this day in His Heavenly forest because the Word of the Lord is right, and all His work is done in truth. He loves righteousness and justice; the earth is full of the goodness of the Lord.

> By the word of the LORD the heavens were made, and all the host of them by the breath of His mouth. [7] He gathers the waters of the sea together as a heap; He lays up the deep in storehouses. [8] Let all the earth fear the LORD; let all the inhabitants of the world stand in awe of Him. [9] For He spoke, and it was done; He commanded, and it stood fast. (Psalm 33:6-9)

How powerful those words written by King David are, and I know they are a timely message for this day and age.

The little sparrow on my lap brings my attention back to him as he begins to chirp the most beautiful sound I have ever heard come from a bird. I believe the sparrow was sent for my enjoyment so I can have the pleasure of listening to a bird that has fallen on earth and now lives in Heaven chirping God's praises. Let everything that has breath praise the Lord!

I sit and listen intently, knowing that I am not to worry about the future as I make my way down the narrow path. The Holy Spirit is reminding me of Jesus' words in Matthew 6:26: "Look at the birds of the air, for they neither sow nor reap nor gather in barns; yet your Heavenly Father feeds them. Are you not of more value than they?"

I thank the sparrow for his kindness and for sharing his love for the Creator with me through his beautiful chirping. Lord, thank you for leading me to this secret place of beauty. I know I must soon leave here and continue my journey down the path. In the forest I see the sweetness of God's glory all around me. "He who dwells in the secret place of the Most High shall abide under the shadow of the Almighty. I will say of the Lord, 'He is my refuge and my fortress; My God, in Him I will trust'" (Psalm 91:1-2).

As the sparrow flies away, I stand to my feet and look around one more time. I close my eyes to savor this moment, for I do not know if I will ever see this place again. As I take a deep breath, my soul inhales and exhales the breath of God and is at peace, for my Creator cares for me. I open my eyes and see a beautiful white swan, larger than a man, flying in the sky. It descends, lands on the water, and glides across the surface to the bank where I am standing. The Holy Spirit prompts me to get on the swan's back, and I do so. The swan lifts from the water, flying me to my next invitation of the Lord. I am excited to see where the swan will take me. As I look around, I can see that the beauty of the Lord's Kingdom is far more beautiful than any words could express. Thank You, Lord, for I trust in You and delight in all Your benefits.

Chapter 9

Strength & Beauty

As I soar high in the air on the swan's back across the majestic fields, rivers, and mountains of Heaven, they all display the strength and beauty that are in His sanctuary. The presence of the King of Glory is in His entire dwelling place. My soul now understands how there are many mansions in my Father's house. I can see a castle in the distance, and though I would love to go there today, I know the Lord has not called me there yet.

I see the banner of love flying over the entire valley below, with sheep in its pastures. The banner of love brings joy to my heart like a rainbow after the rain, showing forth all its brilliant colors because of the promises of God. O Lord, how can I contain all that You are showing me today? My soul has gained strength through the beauty You possess. I look below and see cattle on the hills. I shout with a smile, "My Father owns cattle on a thousand hills!"

How gracefully the swan flies, careful not to lose me. I hear music playing in the air, a melody of instrumental music and angels singing, "Make a joyful shout to the Lord, all you lands! Serve the Lord with gladness; Come before His presence with singing. Know that the Lord, He is God" (Psalm 100:1-3). The Holy Spirit moves in my heart as I began to sing along. and the angels stop singing and let me complete the words. I sing, "It is He who has made us, and not we ourselves; we are the sheep of His pasture. Enter His gates with thanksgiving, and into His courts with praise. Be thankful to Him and bless His name. For the Lord is good; His mercy is everlasting, and His truth endures to all generations" (Psalm 100:3-5).

Listen, O my soul, listen to the sound of love that Heaven must give; it is the love of the Heavenly Father serenading you. I keep glancing below and seeing over and over the strength and beauty of the Lord across the land, and tears of joy fill my eyes. The Lord is our Shepherd, and we are the sheep of His fields. He watches diligently over us. He is our Father and only desires to give us all the good a father can. The benefits of the Lord are more than we can consume.

> The LORD has established His throne in heaven, and His kingdom rules over all. [20] Bless the LORD, you His angels, who excel in strength, who do His word, heeding the voice of His word. [21] Bless the LORD, all you His hosts, You ministers of His, who do His pleasure. [22] Bless the LORD,

all His works, in all places of His dominion. Bless the
LORD, O my soul! (Psalm 103:19-22)

As the swan and I fly over hills and ponds below, I cry out, "I will lift up my eyes to the hills — from whence comes my help? My help comes from the Lord, who made Heaven and earth" (Psalm 121:1-2). Soon, the beautiful white swan gently lands in a body of water and takes me to a dock. I step off the swan onto the wooden dock and thank the swan for flying me to meet my destiny with the Lord. I walk to dry land, looking around and taking in all the wonders of this place, seeing the Lord's beauty and strength radiating from every living thing here. Let my soul inhale and exhale the breath of God in this place.

In this moment, it is easy to understand that He gave me that flight on the swan to refresh my soul. God, you satisfy the longing soul, and You fill the hungry soul with goodness. O God, my heart is steadfast in You. The joy of the Lord is my strength.

Chapter 10

He Who Asks Receives

It was a winter evening, and I had gone to a conference to hear a guest speaker teach us how to make bringing Heaven to earth a lifestyle. I was hungry to learn more. I said, "Heavenly Father, tell me more. I am open to understanding how to do this daily."

Well, that evening the gentleman speaker asked if we were ready to walk into Heaven right where we stood, and of course I was! I stood up, closed my eyes, and listened to his instructions. The man said, "Ask the Holy Spirit to let you see into Heaven's realm. So, I did. Then he said, "When you are ready to go deeper into Heaven, take a step forward." So, I did.

Each step I took, I got deeper into Heaven. Before I knew it, I was clear up to the front of the auditorium, so I finally came to a stop and stood still.

I saw myself walking out of calm water onto a shore. Jesus was standing there, and He invited me into an ancient boat, perhaps like what Peter and the other fishermen used. The boat had no sails. I stepped onto the boat, and it moved away from the shore.

As Jesus and I sailed across the body of water, I moved to the front of the boat, and Jesus came and stood beside me. With His arm around me, we sailed the waters together in silence. I could feel His undying love for me; I felt so much peace and security inside of my soul. I looked at the majestic mountains all around us, the sky a clear and beautiful blue. It seemed that we toured the waters for a long while. Time in Heaven is not like time on earth. In an instant, you can be where you need to be. Then you can return to earth in a blink of an eye. When Jesus returned me to the shore, I hugged Him goodbye. I knew then that I was going to have many more of these moments with my Savior in the future.

That evening, Jesus let me understand these words in a much deeper way than I had ever before: "Ask, and it will be given you; seek, and you will find; knock, and it will be opened to you. For everyone who asks receives, and he who seeks finds, and to him who knocks it will be opened" (Matthew 7:7-8).

Later that evening, the guest speaker gave us another opportunity to step back into Heaven. This time, the Holy Spirit took me to a garden, and Jesus was there waiting for me. We walked up to a bench that overlooked a cliff. As we sat together on the bench, Jesus put His arm around me, and I leaned my head on His shoulders. We sat for a while not saying anything. Jesus knew I just needed His comfort in my soul and spirit.

Our Savior's care for us cannot be fully understood until you sincerely die to yourself and say, "Jesus, I believe You are the true Savior of the world." I am so grateful that Jesus has given His life for me.

Jesus said, "Seek the kingdom of God, and all these things shall be added to you. Do not fear, little flock, for it is your Father's good pleasure to give you the kingdom…For where your treasure is, there your heart will be also" (Luke 12).

Let us never stop asking, that we may receive greater and greater revelations of His kingdom.

Chapter 11

Grace on the Lips

It is time to continue my journey in the good race. As I walk the path, the Holy Spirit leads me to a marble door. Engraved upon it is the word "Grace."

I knock on the door, and it opens to me. I step into a room full of columns, and as I walk down the corridor between them, I see the King of Glory seated on His throne. He lifts His hand toward me, motions for me to come near, and I step forward. Sitting on a short column near the throne is a fire burning in a basin. It is unlike any fire I have ever seen — white with translucent flames and a yellow glow in the center. At the foot of the throne is a step with these words engraved upon it: "He who loves purity of heart, and has grace on his lips, the King will be his friend."

I immediately bow my head, kneel before the King, and begin to weep. For I know there have been times when I have not shown others grace when I should have. As I ask the King's forgiveness, an angel brings out a book and begins reading, "This beloved woman has been a witness to Your grace as she has continued to strive in the good race toward the goal You have put before her. Challenging it may have been, but she is gaining strength through the grace Your Majesty has shown her." I continue to weep, and the King of Glory finally speaks:

"Well done, good and faithful servant. Please stand up, My friend, for I search day and night for those who love a pure heart and who have grace on their lips. I will show them grace, and I welcome their praise before my throne." The music of Heaven begins to play, and before I know it, I am rejoicing in a dance of gratefulness before my King who has forgiven me of all my sins and has shown me grace this day. Bless the Lord, for He is greatly to be praised.

The Holy Spirit of God engulfs me, and I dance with tears of joy before the Lord. The King watches me dance and smiles with tears of joy as well. For He knows my struggles to give grace, but I am an overcomer in Him, and my only desire is to please Him. The Lord seeks those who are willing to give grace, for if we do, we will be called His friends. How can we expect God to give us grace if we do not give it back in the same measure, He has given it to us? O my soul, rejoice, for your King has called you His friend this day because of the grace on your lips.

There was a rich servant of the King that owed money to the royal house, and the King forgave the servant of all his debt. Yet that servant went and beat his servant who owed him money and showed him no grace. When the King heard what the wicked servant had done, he punished him according to the lack of grace he had shown his servant.

How can we win the lost to the Lord if we do not show them the same grace God has shown us through Jesus' death on the cross? The world can only know His grace through those of us who are already the King's friends. Giving grace to others the way the Lord has given it to us loosens the bonds of wickedness and lifts their heavy burdens in the name of the Lord. The grace of the Lord sets the oppressed free, breaking every yoke that has held them in bondage.

Let us step into grace's corridors today and let the spirit of the Lord change our attitudes toward those whom we think may be less deserving of God's grace. I will dance unto the Lord, for He has shown His mercy and grace to me when I was undeserving of it, when I was yet far from Him.

Chapter 12

Depths of the Sea

During my evening prayer time, a window appears. I look out through it and see the Lord standing on a beautiful seashore, and the Holy Spirit tells me to come and be with Him awhile. I turn and walk out the door and onto the sand as Jesus waves for me to come to Him.

In the twinkling of an eye, I am a little girl again. I run barefoot to my Savior as He smiles at me. He takes my hand in His, and we walk for a while, laughing and giggling. Jesus kneels so I can climb up on His shoulders and ride around, pretending He is a horse as he makes playful whinnying sounds. We laugh again and again during our playtime on the seashore. We are to come unto the Lord as little children, and I feel in this moment that Jesus is giving me back all the childhood fun I lost with my earthly father. He restores my soul, for He is a Father to the fatherless.

Jesus bends down to let me off His shoulders. I hop down onto the sand and pick up a seashell, and Jesus and I take turns listening to the call of the sea in the shell's hollow core.

"Jesus, I love being here with you. Where is this place?"

He replies, "Man calls this place the sea of forgetfulness. This is where the Father casts all sin into the depths of the sea."

The wind blows a soft breeze across the shore, and I feel an overwhelming happiness within my soul. I reach up and hug Jesus to show Him my gratefulness for forgiving me of all my sin. I understand in this moment the importance of me coming to Him as a little child on this day by the seashore.

Jesus stands up and reaches out his hand to me to help me up off the sand. "I have a surprise for you," he says. He puts His arm around me, and we walk a short distance to a hammock hanging in between two palm trees. He invites me to lay in the hammock and rest awhile.

While I rest, Jesus sits on a small boulder nearby and asks, "Are you ready for your surprise?" I reply, "Yes, Lord, I am." Jesus calls out to an angel to come with a violin and play music for me while I rest. As the music begins to play, I lie with one leg partially hanging out of the hammock, swinging quietly. As I listen, I fight back tears of thankfulness, praising the Father for His love for me. It is the perfect gift because I love violin music.

My soul soars with the seagulls across the waves of the sea of forgetfulness as the angel plays the violin. I whisper, "Lord, You know everything about me. It is like my first birthday all over again, when my brother played the violin for me. You fill every empty void in my life as only a true friend could."

When the angel finishes playing the violin, I thank him for playing the music for me. I was truly blessed and rested well while listening to the music.

Jesus gently helps me out of the hammock, and we begin our walk back to where we had begun on the seashore. As we walk, I glance down at the glistening sand. It reminds me that I am a part of the promise that God spoke to Abraham when He promised to multiply his descendants like the sand which is on the seashore. For the Lord takes pleasure in His people; He will beautify the humble with salvation, removing our sin as far as the east is from the west, even casting our sin into the depths of the sea. His love for us stretches as high as the heavens are above the earth.

As I depart my time on the seashore with Jesus, I thank Him for making my visit unforgettable.

Chapter 13

Taste & See

One February, I went to a conference in North Carolina to learn more about the Courts of Heaven. The speaker invited everyone to step into Heaven during quiet worship while his wife played the piano. I was eager once again to do so.

My first few steps into Heaven, I heard Jesus ask, "Do you trust me?" I answered, "Yes, Lord." I then took another step into Heaven and heard Jesus ask again, "Do you trust me?" I replied, "Yes, Lord." I opened my eyes and saw that I could not move forward anymore because there was someone standing in front of me. So, I cut through a pew to the left of me to move over to a clear aisle. I then heard the Lord ask once again, "Do you trust me?" I responded, "Yes, I do."

Then Jesus put a blindfold over my eyes and led me to a creature, helping me onto its back. I felt the smooth, slick surface of its back as I straddled it to hold on better. Jesus then pulled the blindfold off me. I could taste and see at that moment that the Lord was good, for He did not want to scare me but needed me to trust Him because of the appearance of the creature.

I was surprised by its features; it looked like something out of *The Wizard of Oz*, and yet I felt perfectly safe on it. The fierce-looking, muscular creature was hairless, with shiny, brownish-red skin, four legs with clawed feet, and a long tail. His head was shaped like a bird's, with a wide, sharp beak for a mouth, and two eyes with dark brown pupils. I knew Jesus would never put me in danger. Then Jesus climbed on the back of another one just like it, and the creatures took off into the air with us on their backs. We flew over mountains, hills, rivers, valleys, and forests. The scenery was stunning. I felt so much freedom as I flew in the air that day on the back of the creature. He looked fierce but was so gentle because of the command of the Lord.

I looked over at Jesus, and we both smiled at each other. I saw several other creatures of the same kind flying behind us in a formation to show respect. I felt so much peace and excitement at the same time because Jesus was taking me on an adventure with Him in the Father's Kingdom. I heard the Holy Spirit say, "These creatures protect the throne of God day and night." I felt such great humility and honor because of the privilege of riding on this incredible creature that has such importance in Heaven before the Lord of glory.

We arrived at a castle — the one I had seen before in the distance while flying on the swan's back. We landed on the rooftop, and Jesus and I dismounted the creatures. In an instant, I was standing in a room at the top of the castle with a beautiful white evening gown on, fit for a princess of the King. My hair was fixed so that it flowed gracefully around my neck. Jesus put a crown on my head, a braided gold belt around my waist, and a gold brooch on my left shoulder. He invited me to look out the window of the castle. I saw the river of life flowing below, surrounded by hills and trees. It was breathtaking. O soul, taste and see that the Lord is good. Inhale and exhale. Breathe, soul, breathe in the breath of God in this place.

When I finally turned away from the window, I was standing in front of a banqueting table. I could not see what was on the table because of the brilliant light that shone from it. Jesus took my hand, and as we both faced the table He said, "This is my daughter Victorious. I am proud of her." Then He told me to wave at those seated there. I kept waving until Jesus motioned for me to stop. I cannot say with enough words how I truly felt at that incredibly special moment with my Savior Jesus. Humility and gratefulness blossomed deep within my soul.

I remained there awhile, until Jesus said it was time to go. The creatures came and got us, and we flew back the way we came. I told Jesus, "I love You, and thank You." I rode on the creature side-saddle, just like a princess would, until I arrived back to where I was when I had walked into Heaven. I slowly opened my eyes and walked back to my seat.

About 30 minutes later, the speaker said, "Everyone stand up and turn to the person next to you." Next, he said, "Hold your hands out toward the person in front of you, without touching them, and pray for them."

Suddenly, the Spirit of the Lord prompted me to pray that the lady in front of me would have the same experience I had at the castle. I told her she was a daughter of the King and how much the Lord loved her. Then the lady started giggling, and we both started laughing with joy at the prophecy I spoke over her.

When I spoke with her the next morning, she told me that in her vision, she had seen another woman fly off on the back of a strange creature. When the woman left, she was straddling it, but when she returned, she was wearing a beautiful white dress and sitting side-saddle like a princess. She even said the creature looked like something from *The Wizard of Oz*!

God is so creative with His messages to us. Putting God in a box to contain Him will not do. He will not have it. His ways and plans are not ours.

Oh, taste and see that the LORD is good; blessed is the man who trusts in Him! 9 Oh, fear the LORD, you His saints! There is no want to those who fear Him. 10 The young lions lack and suffer hunger; but those who seek the LORD shall not lack any good thing. (Psalm 34:8-10)

I will bless the LORD at all times; His praise shall continually be in my mouth. 2 My soul shall make its boast

in the LORD; the humble shall hear of it and be glad. *³ Oh,*
magnify the LORD with me, and let us exalt His name
together. (Psalm 34:1-3)

"The eyes of the Lord are on the righteous" (Psalm 34:15). "The angel of the Lord encamps all around those who fear Him and delivers them" (Psalm 34:7). The radiance of the Lord will shine forth from the saints' faces, and they will not be ashamed.

Wave, soul, wave at the crowd, for you shall not be ashamed to say, "I serve the God of all creation!"

Chapter 14

Breath of God

Later, the speaker at the conference invited us all to step back into Heaven during quiet time worship, while his wife played the piano softly. I was excited to see what the Lord wanted to show me today.

As I stepped into Heaven, I gazed out into space, and the Lord let me see the earth without light. It was just a dark void in space. Then I saw two butterfly-like creatures with arms and legs flying toward the earth. One held up the western side of the earth while another held up the eastern side, as God formed it and all its dwellings therein. Then I saw God move His Spirit across the waters. He breathed His breath into them and told the frozen waters of the earth to wake up because they had an important job to do. He commanded the waters to help Him sustain life on the earth. The waters woke up as God's Spirit moved across them, their frozen darkness awakened. Then, when God was finished, the two butterfly-like creatures flew away. The breath of God had awakened all the earth.

Next, I saw a door appear on the left side of the earth, which God told me to open. When I opened the door, I saw a baby in a mother's womb. The Lord said, "Even while I form a baby in its mother's womb, I have called out that child by name to serve Me." God knows the plans He has for us, for He and He alone will breathe the life of righteousness in us. A generation will rise that will come and declare His righteousness to a people who will be born, and the world will know it was God who did it. He will show us the path of life.

> The earth is the LORD's, and all its fullness, the world and those who dwell therein. ² For He has founded it upon the seas and established it upon the waters. ³ Who may ascend into the hill of the LORD? Or who may stand in His holy place? ⁴ He who has clean hands and a pure heart, who has not lifted up his soul to an idol, nor sworn deceitfully. ⁵ He shall receive blessing from the LORD, and righteousness from the God of his salvation. ⁶ This is Jacob, the generation of those who seek Him, who seek Your face. Selah (Psalm 24:1-6)

Then, in an instant, The Holy Spirit transported me to a beautiful worship room. The floor was made of marble, and I saw a magnificent throne where the Lord Himself was sitting. There was a small pillar, and on it was a basin of fire not known to man. I had seen this fire before in the Grace Room. The fire was a translucent white, with a yellow flame in the center. The Holy Spirit laid upon my heart that the fire represented two tribes spoken of in Obadiah 1:18: "The house of Jacob will be a fire and the house of Joseph a flame." The fire represents all generations that serve the Lord and will be protected by Him.

Then I heard music, and my soul began to dance in one accord with other true worshipers who came and danced with me before the Lord. The fire in the basin seemed to dance along with us. We were in sync with the Holy Spirit of God. I felt so much bountiful love from the Father as I danced with joy before Him. I thanked Him for calling me to be His before I was born; He knew me in my mother's womb and called me out to be set apart for His righteousness.

> *Who is the man that fears the LORD? Him shall He teach in the way He chooses. [13] He himself shall dwell in prosperity, and his descendants shall inherit the earth. [14] The secret of the LORD is with those who fear Him, and He will show them His covenant. [15] My eyes are ever toward the LORD, for He shall pluck my feet out of the net. (Psalm 25:12-15)*

> *One thing I have desired of the LORD, that will I seek: that I may dwell in the house of the LORD all the days of my life, to behold the beauty of the LORD, and to inquire in His temple. [5] For in the time of trouble He shall hide me in His pavilion; in the secret place of His tabernacle He shall hide me; He shall set me high upon a rock. (Psalm 27:4-5)*

And Jesus said, "I shall build my church upon this rock."

As I made my way down the narrow path, I knew I was part of a generation that was prophesied to seek God's face all the days of my life. O soul rejoice that God keeps a fire burning in Heaven before His throne continually as a reminder that He will protect all those who are His.

Chapter 15

I Am the Lord's

I love saying, "I am the Lord's." Being His child, I have a very personal relationship with Him. God has such a wonderful way of showing me Heaven's realm on earth. Whenever I find myself alone and engulfed in deep thoughts of Him, that is when He starts opening Heaven's gate for me. I prepare myself for a most extraordinary, Holy Spirit-packed time with Him.

In the summer of 1978, when I was pregnant with my first son, I was keeping some nieces and nephews for the day. It was around 7:30 in the morning, and all the kids had just gotten to my house. After we said goodbye to their parents, I had the kids go back to bed for a while. Thankfully, the kids were eager to do so. Being pregnant, I needed some extra sleep.

I lay down in bed on my back, and suddenly a cherub angel flew from east to west at the top of my bedroom ceiling. At first, I was shocked; I knew I was not dreaming because I had just gotten in bed.

The angel flew over again, and this time he was moving his lips like he was saying something to me. I could not hear him, only see him. He was a very fierce-looking angel. I am guessing you might not want to mess with him, because he probably could take you out in an instant. Since I could not hear the words, he was speaking to me, I said, "Lord, please let me understand the angel's words."

I fell asleep shortly thereafter. I had a dream that I went to Israel, where I stood on a street made of white stone and spoke with the Lord. In the dream, I saw two young men. One was my son, who would one day visit Israel himself, and the other was my youngest brother. I was to tell my youngest brother that God would give His angels charge to watch over him.

When I woke from this dream, I asked the Lord to give me wisdom about it so I could better understand it, for I had never seen any pictures of Israel before this dream. The Lord showed me that one was for the present and the other was for the future.

First, I called my brother and told him about the dream and the angel I saw. I said, "The Lord wants you to know he is going to give his angels charge over you, and you are not to fear." Later that evening when I saw my brother, he told me that at the time I called him, he was reading the book *The Cross and the Switchblade*. In the very next chapter, he read Psalm 91:11, which declares that "God will command His angels concerning you." He said he had been struggling with whether to go to West Virginia to attend college or not, but he felt that the message I had given him was an answer to his prayer. So, my brother went off to college trusting that the Lord was watching over him and guiding his steps.

Then, several years later, the Lord fulfilled the prophecy that He foretold in the dream. Our second child traveled to Israel in 2005 and blew a shofar on the Temple Mount where no one had blown one in 2,000 years. My husband and I were given an all-expense-paid trip to Israel in 2016, and we lacked nothing while visiting Israel. We are the Lord's, and he watches over us and blesses us beyond what a storehouse can hold.

The Lord says in the book of Isaiah, "I will pour My Spirit on your descendants, and My blessing on your offspring; they will spring up among the grass like willows by the watercourses. One will say, 'I am the Lord's'; another will call himself by the name of Jacob; another will write with his hand, 'The Lord's,' and name himself by the name of Israel" (Isaiah 44:3-5). The book of Micah says, "The remnant of Jacob shall be among the Gentiles" (Micah 5:8).

O soul be joyful, for God is the leader on the narrow path you follow.

Chapter 16

The Scrolls

During my evening quiet time with the Lord, the Holy Spirit leads me into an area of Heaven I have not visited before. I look up and see gold water flowing from a high dwelling place, cascading down a structure that looks like a staircase, and the Holy Spirit leads me up a walkway that runs beside it to the top.

After I reach the top, I am taken into a scribing room where angels keep account of what happens on earth. One angel sits at a scribing machine that has a continuous scroll of paper attached to it. Then the Holy Spirit shows me an ancient-looking wall with an extremely large, crinkled, cloth-like paper cover in colors of red, amber, and brown. It runs from the ceiling to the floor and seems to be a covering and a seal for whatever lies behind it.

An angel lifts the cover to reveal shelves full of scrolls. The angel removes a scroll, sets it on a table, and rolls it open. I look upon the scroll and see hundreds of people, as if they were waves flowing in the sea. Some people belong to the Lord, and others do not, but they are mixed. The words on this page narrate the Parable of the Sower that Jesus tells in the book of Matthew. When the end days arrive and our Heavenly Father returns with our Messiah Jesus, He will send out His angels to pluck the unrighteous from among the righteous on earth and cast them into hell. The righteous will be gathered into God's Kingdom. Learn from the sower, my soul, and seek the Lord while He may be found.

Then the angel retrieves another scroll, lays it on the table, and opens it. As I look upon this scroll, I see a potter working. The potter looks up and smiles at me, and I realize he is Jesus. Jesus is showing me that these scrolls document His and the Father's words that have been spoken from ancient times to the present. These scrolls are about accountability and reveal that all of mankind will be held responsible for their own sins and how they lived or did not live for the Lord.

How captivating that Jesus would remind me of the story of the potter in the book of Jeremiah, when the Father tells Jeremiah that He will give him a message as he watches the potter work. The Lord gives me messages sometimes in a similar matter. It is true, Lord; I am the clay and You are the Potter. You can bend and shape a person any way you want, according to their righteousness or wickedness. Listen, O my soul, the Potter is your Maker, and you are the clay. The Father will bend you into spiritual shape so that you will know everlasting righteousness.

I stay awhile, opening and looking at the scrolls. I feel so much humility in my heart. I am grateful that the Father, Jesus, and the Holy Spirit are my friends. The Father and the Son are One and abide in each other; therefore, they abide in me. Rejoice, my soul, for you are the salt of the earth and a light to the world. Let your light so shine before men that they may see your good works and glorify your Father in Heaven.

As my time ends in the scribing room, I thank the Lord for showing me this place. As I stand up, an angel leads me out and guides me to a large floating device, which I climb into. I ride it down the gentle golden waterfall cascading down toward where I had climbed up from. When I arrive at the bottom, I climb off the floating device and look up toward the top one more time.

In this moment, I know that all of Heaven and Earth are full of God's wisdom. He is the Beginning and the End, and there is no other above Him. And one day all generations will bow and confess with their tongues that Jesus is Lord.

Chapter 17

The Race

I cannot see the finish line. As I run, I see the crowd on both sides of the road cheering me on. I suddenly feel my energy running out and begin to cry. The tears getting heavier, I stagger as I feel myself slowing down, and I feel I am about to faint before long.

Then suddenly, two angels fly up, place themselves on each side of me, and hold me up so I do not dash my foot on a rock and fall to the ground. The Holy Spirit tells me, "Do not give up. You can either cry all the way to the finish line or you can trust the Lord to deliver you." Upon hearing His words of encouragement, I speak out, "I will trust the Lord to deliver me." I speak those words over and over, each time a little louder, until my strength returns. As the angels let go of me, I break into a full run — like a bride running to meet her bridegroom in the night.

In the distance, I see a clocktower, yet there are no hands on the face of the clock. The Holy Spirit speaks these words to me:

"*When* you finish the race is irrelevant; it's about *how* you finish the race."

I am filled with the might of the Lord and begin to run faster than I ever have before.

Suddenly, the creature that flew me to the castle comes flying up behind me, swoops down, and in an instant, I am on his back, flying high in the air with him. From this lofty place, I can now see that I have been wailing and mourning in sackcloth before the Lord. Weeping over people and circumstances I could not change or control. I realize that sometimes the burdens of the world can drag me down. I will trust the Lord to handle all affairs in my life and in the lives of others.

The creature flies me to the forest, and there the Lord turns my ashes into beauty. In the blink of an eye I am back on the creature flying, but this time not in sackcloth. I am wearing the most beautiful wedding dress, fit for a princess of the king. The creature flies me to the castle, where the atmosphere is joyful and festive.

I am whisked to the entryway of a ballroom. Before I enter, a crown is placed on my head, and I hear a voice say, "My beloved is here. I am my beloved's, and she is Mine. I will cherish her from everlasting to everlasting." I feel so much humility and shame because I almost gave up on myself and others while running the race. But in this moment, I know the Lord's wisdom in all my pain, for He will take care of everything I have been concerned about. He could see and hear all things on earth, and He understood my mental anguish over all the problems there. All He wants me to do is have faith to trust Him with the details for myself and others. I cannot carry the burden, for the battle belongs to the Lord. I have learned that I need to trust the Lord for deliverance in all things great and small.

I am grateful that once again the Lord has shown me the love and mercy that only a Father could. He rescues those who are His, and He will deliver them from all their troubles. O soul look up and see how your Heavenly Father adores you.

I hear trumpets, and I enter the ballroom. The same crowd that was cheering me on during the race is now at the ball, and they speak words of blessing upon me as I enter the room. On the floor it is written, "How precious are the feet of the saints." I see Jesus, dressed in formal princely attire. He motions with His head for me to come to Him. I bow in humility, and tears begin to well up in my eyes as I begin my walk toward Him. When I am close enough, He takes my hand in His as I bow my head. He lifts my head up, wipes the tears from my cheeks, and then kisses my hand. Jesus then invites me to dance with Him on the ballroom floor.

My soul is so grateful to be held in the safety of my Savior's arms. It is true that I am my Beloved's and He is mine. Gracefully, we dance across the floor, and all eyes are on us. The crowd is quiet, just watching. Then the music stops, and we both pose in the middle of the dance floor. Jesus says to the crowd, "Tonight I accept Victorious as my bride-to-be." The crowd cheers, and I am overwhelmed with happiness. Then Jesus says, "One day, she will come and live here in the Father's Kingdom as My bride. Until then, we will continue to cheer her on to the finish line."

As quickly as the ball began, it is over. Jesus walks me outside the castle, takes me to a beautiful horse-drawn carriage, and helps me into it. He kisses my hand and waves to the driver to go. I wave goodbye to Him, thanking Him for all the promises He has spoken to me tonight. I will carry them dear to my heart each day as I run the good race.

No man knows the final hour the Lord will return for His bride, the Church. Until then, we must keep our souls ready and prepared to meet the Lord in full wedding attire, for in the blink of an eye He will come. There will be no time to run back and get ready to go, because in a moment He will arrive, sweep His bride off her feet, and disappear into the horizon in His glory. On that day, He will be like a bridegroom coming out of His chambers to race to His bride.

Chapter 18

Prayer Warriors

I t is evening, and I am seeking the Lord, asking what He wants to share with me tonight.

I see a large basin with a flame of fire inside that burns continually in Heaven's prayer room. It represents all the prayer warriors on earth who are constantly sending up their prayers to God's throne room. God is all-seeing and all-knowing. As He sits on His throne, He listens intently to the prayers. The aroma of the prayers sends a sweet fragrance into the air within the room.

I hear voices crying for loved ones who are sick, while others beg for salvation for people they know. Others are praying for cities and nations all over the world. The prayers are constant, and I see ministering angels being sent out to deliver the answered prayers amongst the earth. I see the Lord weep, for the world is in such turmoil, and His heart is broken to see mankind in such aggressive sin and spinning out of control without ever giving Him a thought.

Physical sickness is at an all-time high. The earth and its habitants are in such great need for the King of glory.

God speaks the words written in the book of Isaiah: "Here is the fast I recommend, not one that man likes to boast in so everyone sees and pats him on the back for publicly fasting. Is this not the fast that I have chosen: to loose the bonds of wickedness, to undo the heavy burdens, to let the oppressed go free, and that you break every yoke? Share your bread with the hungry and bring to your house the poor who are cast out. When you see the naked, clothe them. Then your light shall break forth like the morning, your healing shall spring forth speedily, and your righteousness shall go before you; the glory of the Lord shall be your rear guard. Then you shall call, and the Lord will answer; you shall cry, and He will say, 'Here I am'."

As I listen and watch in the prayer room, I hear cheering and celebration in several corridors of Heaven every time a prayer is answered. The sounds of joy and praise to the Lord are all over the halls and Courts of Heaven. O my soul, let us bring joy to our Heavenly Father by doing His fast. The Lord wants us to turn to Him with all our heart. We must rend our hearts to Him, not our garments. God is slow to anger and is full of great kindness.

Before I leave the prayer room, the Lord shows me a map of the world. Some countries have flames burning in them, while others do not. Each flame represents prayers for that nation. The brighter the flame, the more prayers are going up for that nation; the dimmer the flame, the fewer prayers going up. If a nation has no flame, it means no one is praying for that nation.

Lord, give me a praying heart for the lost, the sick, for nations that have no one praying for them. He who claims to live in righteousness must do the true fast of the Lord. May our prayers go up to the prayer room of Heaven and be pleasing to the King of glory. The Lord says, "Call to Me, and I will answer and tell you great and unsearchable things you do not know" (Jeremiah 33:3).

Chapter 19

His Rest

Shabbat is God's way of helping us get the much-needed rest our bodies require after a long week of working, going to school, and doing other activities in our lives. I enter His rest on Friday at sunset and remain in His rest until Saturday at sunset. During my rest, I ask the Holy Spirit to let me see what Shabbat rest is like in Heaven's realm.

I soon see a garden, where the Father is walking with His Son on the paths that lead through it. There is complete quietness as all in the garden is resting. There is a brook, and the water has slowed to a soft trickle.

I see the Father and His Son walk to a bench, sit down, and visit quietly amongst themselves. After a while, the Son stands up, bids His Father farewell, and continues down another path in the garden. The Father lies down on the bench and closes His eyes to rest.

Soon, an angel approaches Him and says, "There is a call from earth that requires attention. Shall I send out a messenger to handle the situation?"

The Father says, "No, the crisis will still be there after our rest period is over, and nothing with the situation will change before then."

The angel replies, "I agree, it seems the situation could have been avoided if Shabbat rest would have been applied as Your commandment requires." The Father nods His head and lies back down on the bench to continue His rest.

The Holy Spirit lets me see into other places in Heaven, and I see that all is quiet and resting while the Father is resting. Heaven has such breathtaking scenery. There are mountains, rolling hills, rivers, streams, ponds, brooks, fields with animals of all kinds, and gardens with birds and small wildlife in them. I can see that God absolutely loves nature. All these places reveal the beauty and peace of our Father's creativity in its forever splendor.

I walk along the narrow path in Heaven's garden, looking about with curiosity. Like a child in a candy store, I take in as much as I can in this precious moment. I stop along the path, sit beside the brook flowing alongside it, and can smell the aroma of all the flowers and other vegetation that are pleasing to the soul. Oh, my soul, take rest in the Father's Shabbat.

In Heaven, there is really no need for shoes because there are no stones, stickers, or other dangers that could harm you. God runs His

Kingdom with great care and takes pleasure in all His creation, great and small. Our Father in Heaven is a master at farming, agriculture, and the engineering of all things. His wisdom is beyond what man could ever envision.

As I rest, my soul inhales and exhales the breath of life from my Creator in this wondrous place in Heaven. How can it be that I am so loved by my Heavenly Father that He seeks to give me only good from the bounty of His treasury?

I hear my Father arousing from His rest in the garden, and I hear Him call out, "Victorious, come to Me." I stand up and walk the path to Him, like a child giggling with excitement that my Father desires to speak with me. My slow walk increases to a fast walk, and as I round the bend of the path, there my Father awaits me. I sit beside Him, thank Him for Shabbat rest, and ask forgiveness for not always observing His day of rest. He encourages me to learn from my mistake and to go forth to teach others to rest on Shabbat. I reach out to embrace my Father, and His love engulfs me. And in a moment, I am back, sitting before my computer, leaving Heaven's Shabbat to start a fresh work week with the Lord's guidance in full rest that pleases Him.

Let us be reminded of the fourth commandment of the Lord:

Remember the Sabbath day, to keep it holy. ⁹ Six days you shall labor and do all your work, ¹⁰ but the seventh day is the Sabbath of the LORD your God. In it you shall do no work: you, nor your son, nor your daughter, nor your male servant, nor your female servant, nor your cattle, nor your stranger who is within your gates. [11] For in six days the LORD made the heavens and the earth, the sea, and all that is in them, and rested the seventh day. Therefore, the LORD blessed the Sabbath day and hallowed it. (Exodus 20:8-11)

Jesus said, "I did not come to do away with the law, but to fulfill it" (Matthew 5:17). In other words, what we could not do on our own by obeying the Ten Commandments, we now can. Jesus said He would not leave us as orphans, but He would send the Comforter, the Holy Spirit, who helps us to obey God's Word with wisdom, knowledge and understanding. This means we are no longer powered by our own flesh, but by His Spirit.

Chapter 20

The Rainbow

My husband John and I own a painting business. One evening, I had to go visit with a customer and close out the final paperwork on their home project. Afterward, as I was driving home, I decided to drive by the cemetery and check on my older sister's grave.

I parked the car and walked down to her grave. Standing there quietly for a moment, I whispered, "I miss you, sister."

After I walked back to the car and got in, I rolled down the passenger window so I could play her favorite song and just sit listening to the words. I became overwhelmed with sorrow and began to cry. I thought of how happy my sister must be in Heaven, yet I still felt that human selfishness swell up within me. I wanted my sister here on earth, with me.

I said, "Lord, I miss my sister, my friend, so much. There is such a deep void and empty space in my life now without her." The pain in my heart was great.

When I finally gained my composure, I drove out of the cemetery gate and started on the road home. In just a short distance, I had to stop at a red light and began to cry again. At that very moment, the Lord whisked me away into Heaven, and I saw the most beautiful rainbow I had ever seen. The colors in it were so brilliant that the Lord had to soften the colors so they would not hurt my eyes. If you have ever had a colored water drink in a wax bottle when you were a kid, like I did, you will understand the brilliant hues of each color in the rainbow.

The Holy Spirit led me across a path that brought me directly up to the rainbow. Then I was instructed to walk up onto it, and I walked with ease to the top. The rainbow was extremely large, and in earth time, it might have taken me several hours to make it to the top. But in Heaven time, it was but a moment.

In the blink of an eye, I was back in my car. The red light had turned green, and I continued driving down the road home. When I arrived, I could not stop thinking about the Heavenly rainbow. I kept praying and asking the Lord why He had let me see it. He did not answer my question until the next morning while I was getting ready for work.

My younger brother who lives in Houston called me, and he and I got into a conversation about God and the visions He gives us. I told him I had finished 20 chapters in my new book and had quit listening to Christian programs or reading Christian books, because I did not want programs or books to influence what the Lord wanted me to write about. My brother encouraged me not to do that, but to keep watching and reading, so God could give me a message like He did with Jeremiah when he went to the potter's house.

After hanging up, I quickly opened the Christian app on my phone, which had a story of a four-year-old girl who visits Heaven often, like I do. She has seen several rainbows there and described the same rainbow I saw in Heaven the day before — huge, but with muted hues because its colors were too bright for human eyes. Reading her story was confirmation of the encouragement my brother had given me to not deprive myself of all the ways God can speak to me while writing my book.

I turned off the app on my phone and started thanking the Lord for letting me hear her story. It encouraged me to press in more with Holy Spirit and find out why I was shown the rainbow. I said, "Lord, I am ready to see what is at the top of the rainbow."

In a quick second, there I was standing on top of the rainbow. The Holy Spirit said, "Look out across the left side of the rainbow and tell me what you see." I turned my head to the left and saw the most beautiful city ever imaginable. It was made of a solid white substance, but it was not stone. There were no visible lines or connecting points on the buildings. Each structure was made of a continuous material without lines. In the center, there was a tower that looked out over the entire city. It had an ornate window with an arch at the top of it, and its roof rose high into a point like a castle. Even its shingles were white. On the point of the roof, there was a pole with a banner flag attached, flying in the wind. The words written upon it read, "Living it up with God."

As my eyes scanned the city, I saw double doors open on a balcony and heard music playing from its inner room. Then I saw a person walking toward the balcony's edge and did a double take, not quite believing my eyes.

It was my sister, whose grave I had visited the day before. She began to wave at me, smiling. I began to cry overwhelming tears as she said, "Valerie Valentine, my sweet sister who is called and known by 'Victorious' throughout all of Heaven, do not cry for me, for I am living it up with God now. This is my mansion. What do you think of my new place?"

I could not help but smile and cry at the same time. For this was the mansion my sister had always known she would live in once she left earth to live her everlasting life with the Lord. As I laughed and cried at the same time, I saw her smiling and laughing with me, showing me her full set of beautiful teeth, she had always dreamed of having but could not afford on Earth.

I finally said, "I miss you greatly, but I am so happy for you. I am so happy for you. I knew all along you were okay, but I am still selfish in wanting you with me on earth."

She replied, "I understand, sister, but it will all be okay. Please do not cry for me, for I am with the Lord and living it up with Him every day now. One day, you will fully understand what Heaven is all about. Keep searching His Kingdom secrets because He will keep revealing them to you. I am proud of you, sister; please tell everyone I heard what they each said to me at the hospital on the day I passed over and walked into Heaven in a blink of an eye. I was standing in the realm of Heaven with the angel of the Lord and had asked if I could see my family one more time before I left for Heaven. God said yes. I did not want to go until I heard everyone in my family say their goodbyes to me."

I was exceedingly joyful to see my sister. Thank You, Lord, for letting me visit and see her. I am grateful that she lives with You. I thank the Father for comforting me. My sister says, "Oh, one more thing. Please tell my dear, precious husband that I love him and do not want him to be hard on himself. He made me happy all the days of my life while we were married, and one day we will see each other again. Until then, chin up." As she turns to go back indoors, she smiles and points up to the banner flying high on the tower, saying, "That is the name I chose for my mansion." She waves to me one more time and blows me a kiss before walking back through the double doors on the balcony and disappearing.

I wanted to spend longer talking with my sister, but I knew it was time for me to continue my journey back down the rainbow. I am called to a journey on earth for now, and until I live in Heaven, I must run the good race the Lord has assigned to me. In Heaven there are no tears of sorrow, only tears of joy. How funny that what I thought was a city was my sister's mansion in Heaven! Wow, Lord, if that is my sister's mansion, I cannot wait to see mine.

Jesus says He goes to prepare a place for us in Heaven, and in His Father's house are many mansions. Oh my soul, be comforted and know that the Lord cares about your sorrows and only wants to turn your weeping into joy. The Lord says to those who obey His commandments, "Blessed shall you be when you come in, and blessed shall you be when you go out" (Deuteronomy 28:6).

The Holy Spirit instructed me to go down the other side of the rainbow, find the narrow path, and begin a new phase of my journey that would be unlike anything I had seen before. And I obeyed.

Chapter 21

The Blue Path

I do not descend the rainbow as quickly as I ascended it. The Lord has me go slower and take my time. When I am about halfway down the rainbow, He says, "Choose a color from the rainbow, and that will be the next path I have you travel." I feel drawn to the blue, so I walk to that color. I stand in the vast, vibrant color of blue and wait upon the Lord to tell me my next step. I can clearly see that the Lord loves vibrant colors, and it means so much to me to be able to stand in a rainbow, a visible promise that He will never again destroy the earth by flood.

Oh Father, it is true, you do show those who seek You the most wonderful secrets of Heaven not known to man. I feel Heaven deep within me, and I tell my soul once again to inhale and exhale the breath of God in this rainbow. Sparkles of Heaven are suspended in the air all around me while I stand in the blue color of the rainbow. Sleep comes over me, and when I awake, I am lying under a tree in Heaven, with the blue path right in front of me.

I stand to my feet and begin to walk on the translucent blue path, peering at the ground beneath through the rich color. I can see that the Lord has enlarged my path so my feet do not slip. I continue to walk, admiring the beauty of Heaven all around me, and I soon come to a large stone along the path where I sit down to pause and rest for a while.

I finally stand to my feet, continue my journey down the path, and come upon a field with a sign that reads, "Field of Words." Then an angel appears and says, "This field is where the words spoken on earth are cultivated and loosed in Heaven. Therefore, take care how you speak on earth, for life and death are in the tongue." I am astounded as I realize I have been guilty of speaking wrong things with my mouth, and I ask the Lord to forgive me.

I walk a bit further and come upon a field of pillars, where an angel appears and says, "This is the Field of Promises, which represents all the promises God spoke to His people Israel. He has not failed to keep one of them, even when Israel failed in their promises to Him." I immediately repent because I understand what the angel means. When we fail God, He never fails us. He will never retreat from His spoken promises, no matter what. He is a God of integrity.

I walk a bit further on the path and see a Field of Doors, where another angel appears and says, "These doors represent the calling of the Lord on people's lives all across the earth, and they are waiting to be opened. The doors will not open until the person answers the call of the Lord, for many are called, but few are chosen." I feel so much remorse and ask forgiveness, remembering that there was a time when I did not answer the call of the Lord.

God tells us to call to Him, and He will answer. Whoever answers the Lord's call will not be ashamed, for the fullness of the Lord will fill our new wineskins with all we need to be equipped for ministry or anything else he calls us to. Fear not, for the Lord is with you.

As my time on the blue path comes to an end, I see another path that is white and leads to a castle in the distance. I will follow that path as the Holy Spirit of the Lord leads. Thank you, Father, for calling me. I have answered the call, and I am ready for the next adventure with you.

Chapter 22

The Path of White

I cross from the blue path onto the path of white and wonder where the Lord will lead me next. As I walk this path, I look in wonder at the sweetness of Heaven all around me, shimmering as far as my eyes can see. I can still see in the far distance the beautiful white castle, yet I do not know if the Lord will allow me to go there while I travel this new path. Lord, You are so amazing. You truly have shown me your wonders, and I am grateful no matter where You take me.

I travel down the path of white and come upon a bridge, with water flowing beneath it. I walk along the bridge and look below into the water, where I see the reflection of an angel standing behind me. The angel says to me, "Every time you answer the call of the Lord, another door in Heaven opens for you."

Obedience truly is better than sacrifice. I tell the angel that I understand and will put forth a great effort to always answer the call of the Lord. The angel then says that he has been instructed to stay with me until I reach the end of the path of white. So, I continue down the path with the angel as my rear guard.

As I walk, I see a violin leaning on a door, which the angel instructs me to pick up. "Now, play it," the angel says, and as I put the violin to my chin and touch the bow to the strings, I begin to play the most soul-healing music I have ever heard. As I continue to play the violin, I see true worshipers come and line the path of white and begin to sing praises to the Lord of glory. I walk down the center of them and continue to play the violin, and we all lift praises to the Father as one. All of Heaven worships in one accord, and the power of Heaven's unity is like none on earth. I leave the true worshipers as I continue down the path playing the violin, and I arrive at a cove with still waters and green pastures.

I see a man robed in white, with a crown on his head, and he is playing the tune of Psalm 23 on a small handheld harp. He smiles at me and nods his head as we play our string instruments in unison.

I realize I have just met King David, the creator of the music we are playing. I feel so much humility that the Lord would allow me to meet such a saint like King David. After we stop playing Psalms 23, he motions for me to come over and talk to him.

He tells me that in Heaven he is not known as King David anymore, for there is only one King in Heaven and it is not him. I smile and agree with him. David says to me, "Victorious, the return of the Messiah is near, and He will use you to tell the message. You have a heart after God's own heart, and He knows that even through your struggles you do not waver in your devotion to Him. You must stay strong and use the wisdom of the Lord to help guide you down the narrow path. Like God did with me, God has chosen you because of your heart before Him. Stay pure in heart, and greater things He will show you."

Then David tells me, "The path of white you are on is the path of righteousness." I fall to my knees weeping, for many times on earth I have not felt worthy of the One who saved me from all my sins. I feel a hand touch me on my head, and I look up to see Jesus, the righteous Branch of David. Jesus helps me up, and with the angel of the Lord as our rear guard, the three of us begin to walk down the path of righteousness together.

David and Jesus walk on each side of me, offering me their arms, which I gladly accept as we set off toward the castle. Before I know it, we arrive, and David says, "Victorious, this castle is mine." I smile and say, "I should have known." I let him know what an honor it is to meet him, and as I hug him goodbye and thank him for his hospitality, he says, "We'll meet again one day." I see engraved on the wall of his castle, "The Lord is my Shepherd."

Jesus and I wave goodbye and continue down the path of righteousness together, for the Lord is my Shepherd and goes with me; in Him I will trust and lack nothing.

Chapter 23

The Path of Righteousness

It is a Saturday evening Shabbat in August, and I am outside sitting on the swing on my back porch, listening to instrumental music that inspires my soul. It rains lightly as I watch the clouds form different shapes in the sky. I hear thunder in the distance as another storm rolls in.

The Lord lays upon my heart to pray for a specific U.S. state and country. As I pray, I ask the Lord to tell me more about the path of righteousness. Sitting in the swing, I close my eyes and focus on Him.

Soon, Jesus appears. We walk off together into the sky and sit on a cloud. With our feet dangling off the cloud, Jesus and I exchange small talk and laugh with one another, like friends do together. Once the small talk is over, Jesus says, "As you continue the path of righteousness, you will quickly learn to see and hear what I do and why I do it. I only say and do what my Father does; therefore, you will continue to learn to walk in His righteousness."

While Jesus speaks these words to me, He transports us to a city street on earth. It is evening as He and I walk past the homeless sitting and lying on the sidewalk. As we walk down the path of injured souls, several of them yell or scream as demons of all sorts flee out of the people.

A man yells, "Jesus, save me!" And Jesus kneels and touches the man's forehead with such gentle compassion. He heals the man of alcoholism, and the man becomes sound of mind instantly. The man stands to his feet and thanks Jesus for setting him free from all the demons that kept him bound. Jesus tells the man to go and share with others what God has done for him this day and then says, "Now go, and do not fall into the trap of sin anymore." The man walks off into his new life in Christ.

Soon, we come upon a blind man. Jesus spits on His hand, mixes it with dirt, and puts the mud mixture on the man's eyes. The man opens his eyes and says, "Jesus has broken the chains of bondage that held me bound." Jesus smiles as the man picks up his flute and begins to play a song of worship to the Lord.

We continue our walk through the crowd of the homeless. Next, a woman screams, "It is the Son of God!" A demon flees her body, and she is set free instantly. She thanks Jesus for making her whole again. He says, "Woman, go and sin no more." With a grateful soul, she walks down the sidewalk and out of sight.

All of sudden, I understand what Jesus is teaching me. He wants me to have compassion for the lost. Jesus reminds me that even if a man has 100 sheep and one is lost, he will leave the 99 and go after the one that is lost.

I continue to follow Jesus through the crowd of homeless people and see that even when His shadow falls on a person, they are set free. Where the Spirit of the Lord is, there is liberty. Jesus says to me, "My sheep hear my voice, and they answer when I call. I am the Good Shepherd; I know my sheep and am known by my own. The love that the Father has loved Me with, may it be in them, as I dwell in them."

Tears fill my eyes because I see how merciful our Father in Heaven is to those who are lost. It brings him no joy to punish the wicked. Behold, the Lamb of God has come to save the world. May the Lord give those of us who are His a true hunger to give a lost and dying world a chance to hear His call, so they may know the same love the Father He has shown all of us. Lord, may we have the boldness to help others follow the path of righteousness.

Chapter 24

God Widens the Path

My friend Brandy and I sit at my kitchen table one Sunday afternoon, visiting and praying. One of the subjects we discuss is the narrow path that God's word talks about and how each of us must learn to follow that path. We talk about how God widens the path beneath us, so we do not slip.

Then Brandy and I conclude that one of the Kingdom secrets is that God widens the narrow path beneath us as we continue on it, until eventually the narrow path transforms into the wide path that God promises to us in Psalm 18:36. In fact, God widens the narrow path so much that it even overtakes the wide path that leads to destruction!

God wants to reveal His Kingdom secrets to those who ask, seek, and knock. He will let you find the truth that sets your soul's compass on the correct course toward the everlasting wisdom that only He can give. Then you will find the hidden treasures in His word that will forever change your life.

As you grow and mature on the narrow path, you will gain much wisdom, knowledge, and understanding from the Holy Spirit. Ask the Holy Spirit to show you what is on your narrow path and comfort you while on that path so you can start learning and seeing Kingdom secrets. Walking on the narrow path is not for the faint of heart. As you get serious about serving the Lord and staying on the path of righteousness, you cannot help but let God start transforming your heart into a new creation in Christ.

God is in the business of changing and transforming people into powerhouses for Him. You will be like a lighthouse on a cliff shining its light into the darkness so others can see their way to the narrow path, to live in righteousness before the Father. All God asks of us is to follow the narrow path so He can widen His path beneath us. As the path widens, we can receive the overflowing blessings He has stored up for us.

Bless the Lord, oh my soul, for you seek the King of glory, whose benefits restore and heal all the struggles in your life. Hallelujah, bless the Lord, for He is the keeper of the narrow path.

Lord, I have chosen to follow You. I will not look to the right or to the left so that I can remain undistracted from Your call on my life. I will make a conscious decision today to lay down my life, take up my cross, and follow You.

Blessed be the name of the Lord, for He is the God who watches over my soul. He widens my path so that it can be soaked in His care, full of so many blessings that I cannot contain them all. Follow, soul, follow, for the King of Righteousness stands at the door and knocks. Invite Him in, and He will sup with you from everlasting to everlasting. Today is here, and tomorrow may not come; there is no time to waste. Seek the Lord while He may be found, for we are not promised tomorrow.

Chapter 25

The Witness

It is evening when I finally return to my quiet time with God. I thumb through my Bible, asking the Lord to speak. The Lord begins speaking to me about people who want to pretend in their walk with Him. They are trying to "fake it 'til they make it." They pretend they have all the answers, yet they have none, and they keep asking spiritual questions but have not advanced in their spiritual walk and relationship with the Lord.

Does God's Spirit bear witness in you, and you in Him?

Many times, Jesus was judged by people who constantly tried to catch Him in a lie or make Him look bad in front of others. Jesus was great at using wisdom in His spoken words that made those people look foolish. Let us go back in time, with Jesus at the center of attention.

The Pharisees wanted to trap Jesus by saying, "You bear witness of yourself; your witness is not true" (John 8:13). Jesus replied:

Jesus answered and said to them, "Even if I bear witness of Myself, My witness is true, for I know where I came from and where I am going; but you do not know where I come from and where I am going. ¹⁵ You judge according to the flesh; I judge no one. ¹⁶ And yet if I do judge, My judgment is true; for I am not alone, but I am with the Father who sent Me. ¹⁷ It is also written in your law that the testimony of two men is true. ¹⁸ I am One who bears witness of Myself, and the Father who sent Me bears witness of Me." (John 8:14-18)

And of course, the Pharisees could not stop at one question; they had to ask him, "Where is your Father?" Jesus answered, "You know neither Me nor My Father. If you had known Me, you would have known My father also" (John 8:19).

Jesus trapped them in their own law. They said two men had to provide a witness. Jesus wisely replied that He and His Father are two, and the Father bore witness for him. Therefore, what Jesus said was true. He let them know that by their questions, He knew they were not saved.

Jesus said, "I am going away, and you will seek me, and will die in your sin. Where I go you cannot come" (John 8:21). Why did Jesus say this? Because God the Father is Spirit, and we must serve Him as such. We must look beyond our earthly thinking to understand the Kingdom secrets. If we are true witnesses in the Father, then we will know when the truth is spoken in His name.

So the Jews said, "Will He kill Himself, because He says, 'Where I go you cannot come'?" ²³ And He said to them, "You are from beneath; I am from above. You are of this world; I am not of this world. ²⁴ Therefore, I said to you that you will die in your sins; for if you do not believe that I am He, you will die in your sins."

²⁵ Then they said to Him, "Who are You?" And Jesus said to them, "Just what I have been saying to you from the beginning. ²⁶ I have many things to say and to judge concerning you, but He who sent Me is true; and I speak to the world those things which I heard from Him." ²⁷ They did not understand that He spoke to them of the Father. ²⁸ Then Jesus said to them, "When you lift up the Son of Man, then you will know that I am He, and that I do nothing of Myself; but as My Father taught Me, I speak these things. ²⁹ And He who sent Me is with Me. The Father has not left Me alone, for I always do those things that please Him." (John 8:22-29)

You and the Father are one, and you are true witnesses upon the earth. How can we judge the spiritual matters of God if we are not His and not walking a Spirit-filled life? It is simple: we cannot.

The Father is calling you today. How will you answer back to Him? I beg you: If you are seeking the Lord, now is the time of your salvation. Stop a moment and ask Jesus to forgive you of all your sins. Then invite Him into your heart to be your Savior, and He will. It is that simple. Next, ask Jesus to fill you with His Holy Spirit, and

He will. It is that simple. God is not a feeling. He is a spirit, and therefore we must get to know him as such.

The word says that if you deny Jesus in front of men, Jesus will deny you in front of the Father (Matthew 10:33). How can we know the truth, unless we accept the One who can set us free from all our sins? Jesus has overcome the world for us; therefore, we must make Him Lord over all in our life. Greater is He who is in me than he who is in the world. If you have accepted the Lord in your heart today, thank Him for coming to abide in you. Make living for the Lord a lifestyle. We cannot put Him on a coat hook and take Him down when we want to.

I love living for the Lord. He gives my life peace and purpose. Whether you are a new Christian or have been one for years, we must make living for the Lord our number one priority. If we seek His Kingdom first and His righteousness, then all will fall into order in our life. The narrow path leads to righteousness, and the wide path leads to destruction. Jesus said, "These things I have spoken to you, that in Me you may have peace. In this world you will have tribulation; but be of good cheer, I have overcome the world" (John 16:33).

Jesus prayed for believers, saying, "I pray for them. I do not pray for the world but for those whom You have given Me, for they are Yours. And all Mine are Yours, and Yours are Mine, and I am glorified in them. Now I am no longer in the world, but these are in the world, and I come to You. Holy Father, keep through Your name those whom You have given Me, that they may be one as We are."

Chapter 26

Valley of Decision

I find myself walking in a desolate place. I come upon a great divide and do not know what I am supposed to do. As I stand and look in wonder, I hear the voice of an angel say, "You have come to the Valley of Decision. Now move forward." I obey.

A bridge appears, and I walk over it. The angel says, "God uses prophets to build bridges between Him and man. A prophet must help encourage man to cross over the Valley of Decision and live for God. Those who do not cross over will not be written in the Lamb's Book of Life." The Lord is calling out true shepherds to lead his flock to serve the Lord of Righteousness. I hear the voice of the Lord say, "The days are near that I will not withhold my anger against the earth, and I will strike it and cause a shaking like never before known to man. The earth is in its final days. I will cause a great divide, and man will only have a moment as quick as a lightning strike to decide about who he will serve. A servant cannot serve two masters; he will either love one or hate the other. The day is coming when My people who have chosen Me will no longer call Me master, but their husband, for I will not relent from My word."

I stand in fear and trembling, for I know it is a message I must bring to the nations. My Father in Heaven has spoken as He did in the ancient days to all of Israel; I must help the lost find their way to the Lamb of God. God has spoken in His word that the sacrifice He wants from man is from his lips, asking forgiveness of all his iniquities. When we offer this sacrifice, He will heal man's backsliding ways and will love him freely with His lovingkindness and show him mercy, for the Lord takes joy in showing grace.

How will the Lord do this for the nations? "Not by might, nor by power, but by my Spirit," says the Lord Almighty. We as believers must be attentive to the voice of the Lord and learn how to discern His voice between the worlds. God desires to answer the call of His sheep and loves for us to put Him to the test to see if He will answer.

I walk over the bridge and see a rocky path by the side of a hill. As I follow this winding path, I step into a clearing. There is a gate that leads into a garden, which I enter. I follow a path lined with all kinds of beautiful flowers and hear birds chirping and water softly flowing nearby. I walk slowly on the path, admiring the beauty in this garden.

Arriving at an open body of water, I see a small white boat near the shore. I look up to see an angel in a cloud, who drops an anchor down. As the anchor falls into the water, I notice that it is not attached to the boat. The angel instructs me to get into the boat, and

I obey. Six angels appear, three on each side of the boat, and they travel with me to my next destination. We arrive at a new shore that is lined with tall, beautiful purple flowers swaying in the wind.

I step on to the shore and view the splendor of this place. I know a new phase is about to begin with the Lord as I travel the path of righteousness. I turn to look at the angels, but they have disappeared. So, I walk up the shore on a path alone, and it leads into deep, beautiful vegetation. The path leads into a garden, and I see now why the Lord brought me to this place.

The Holy Spirit speaks to me and says, "See the beauty of this garden; it is like no other in all of Heaven or earth." It is God's favorite because every time He heals the desolate heart of a man, He adds a new created plant or flower to this garden, making it the most flourishing, beautiful, and largest of all His gardens. Seeing this place, I know God can turn a man's dry heart into a Garden of Eden as His word says He can. I feel so humbled that the Lord has seen fit to bring me to His most cherished garden.

Spotting a bench close by, I walk over to it and sit down. I look all around and admire the extraordinary splendor of this garden. I thank the Father for His great love He has shown mankind and His enduring patience.

Jesus comes and sits with me. He tells me He wants me to keep sharing about the Father's love to others and sound the alarm to all the nations that He is returning, and man must seek Him while He may be found. As He speaks, I sense the Lord's sweetness toward mankind and His deep desire to not condemn the world. His love can cover a multitude of sins. I tell Jesus I will share His message.

When a person arrives at the Valley of Decision, they will only be shown the bridge to cross over to God's Kingdom based on their heart before the Lord. Faith is the substance of things hoped for; therefore, the Lord is calling the world into order in His court. The word of God says:

"Listen to Me, you who follow after righteousness, You who seek the LORD: look to the rock from which you were hewn, and to the hole of the pit from which you were dug. ² Look to Abraham your father, and to Sarah who bore you; for I called him alone, and blessed him and increased him." ³ For the LORD will comfort Zion, He will comfort all her waste places; He will make her wilderness like Eden, and her desert like the garden of the LORD; joy and gladness will be found in it, thanksgiving and the voice of melody. ⁴ "Listen to Me, My people; and give ear to Me, O My nation: for law will proceed from Me, and I will make My justice rest as a light of the peoples. ⁵ My righteousness is near, My salvation has gone forth, and My arms will judge the peoples; the coastlands will wait upon Me, and on My arm they will trust. ⁶ Lift up your eyes to the heavens and look on the earth beneath. For the heavens will vanish away like smoke, the earth will grow old like a garment, and those who dwell in it will die in like manner; but My salvation will be

forever, and My righteousness will not be abolished. (Isaiah 51:1-6)

God's righteousness will be forever, His salvation from generation to generation. Listen up, oh my soul, and search, search for the One who is and is to come. May the Lord's name be lifted up and honored for all ages to come. For one cannot trust in his own beauty but can trust in the beauty of the Lord's mercy.

Lord, please cultivate Your Garden of Eden in all areas of my soul that are dry and without You.

Chapter 27

Who Do You Say I Am?

For a couple of days, I kept seeing a vision of faces and wondered why I was seeing them. During my quiet time with the Lord on a Sunday evening, I ask the Holy Spirit to reveal to me who the faces are.

I hear the Lord ask, "Who do you say I am?" Suddenly, I connect the dots of the story He wants to tell me. The world is in an identity crisis and suffering from the rot of sin. The people not only cannot tell who they are, but they cannot tell Jesus who He is. This means Satan is pushing forward in the final hour to take down as many people as he can, because he knows his final day is fast approaching. Therefore, if he can bring utter confusion to people and make them believe there is no God, then they will not understand who they are and why they were created or who created them. Is it then possible that Satan has won half the battle, unless a righteous believer steps in and says, "Enough is enough," and speaks out, "It is written that man shall not live by bread alone, but by every word that proceeds out of the mouth of God"?

Let us go to the highways and byways to reach the lost for Christ. Let us teach the children of all lands far and wide about Who created them, who they are, and why they were created. Forgive me, Father, for I am guilty of not doing my share to spread Your identity message through the gospel.

In a moment, I am reminded of my visit to Jerusalem in 2016. I see myself walking with the tour group on a stone street in Jerusalem, following the path that Jesus took to Calvary. It is rainy and cold. I am holding an umbrella and complaining in my heart.

The next morning, as I get ready to go on another tour, the Holy Spirit convicts my heart about all the complaining I did the day before. The Holy Spirit says, "You only had to carry an umbrella, but Jesus had to carry a cross and receive beatings as He walked the path to die for your sins at Calvary. Now tell me again, why did you have the right to complain?" I feel so much shame and embarrassment before the Father, so I repent and do not complain anymore during the trip but continue with a grateful heart.

We as believers in Jesus must be able to reach a lost and dying world that has lost its way. We must be able to answer the question, "Who do you say I am?" Like Simon Peter, we must be able to answer, "You are the Christ, the Son of the living God." How will the world know who Jesus is, if we do not know?

Jesus answered and said to him, "Blessed are you. Simon Bar-Jonah, for flesh and blood has not revealed this to you, but My Father who is in heaven. [18] And I also say to you that you are Peter, and on this rock, I will build My church, and the gates of Hades shall not prevail against it. [19] And I will give you the keys of the kingdom of Heaven, and whatever you bind on earth will be bound in Heaven, and whatever you loose on earth will be loosed in Heaven." (Matthew 16:17-19)

We have been given the keys of the kingdom of Heaven to break the bondage of the identity crisis that holds the world captive. The first key is to use the word of God because it is sharper than any two-edged sword; it will destroy the plans of the enemy to confuse the world. We are fearfully and wonderfully made and are created to worship our Heavenly Father. He created us because He wanted to have communion and friendship with us. He is a God of freedom. That is why where the Spirit of the Lord is, there is liberty. He who is in the Lord is free indeed.

Chapter 28

Sun, Be Still

It is a Tuesday evening, and I am listening to a man on the computer speak about his new book on prophecy of things to come. As I sit and listen, I hear the voice of the Holy Spirit say, "Run, run, now jump and dive into the air."

As I obey, I find myself in between space and time. I am floating in the air, looking around at an area that seems to be an air pocket in time. It is a strange new area I have not visited before, and I look around in awe of this place. I sense that here, time is still, and it reminds me of Joshua telling the sun and moon to stand still while he fought the battle against his enemy. Joshua's words show how powerful our words can be when we use our authority in the Lord.

Time is of the essence when we are in the midst of a spiritual battle. What God did for Joshua He will do for us who are His. Time can stand still for us when God has an important battle for us to overcome. If we will only believe, God will do above and beyond our wildest imagination to help us win the victory in any battle small or great. For it is the battle within we must win.

If finding time with God is a big issue for you, then ask God to give you wisdom in how to better manage it. Let us take a lesson from Joshua saying, "Sun, be still; moon, be still." The word "still" must have more power than we think because Jesus said to a raging sea storm, "Peace! Be still!" There is power in that word, "still," and that is why the Lord says to be still and know He is God.

If we are in a constant storm in our life, then we must find the eye of the storm so we can have stillness and hear the Lord speak to us, which will help us move forward without distraction. Listen, soul, listen. Ask God how to redeem the time so you can reach further into His quietness that holds a glorious destiny for you.

As I float in the air pocket of no time, I sense the Holy Spirit telling me that the key to understanding this Kingdom secret of being still is much greater than I know. I see a vision of clock gears that govern the sun and moon, and I see the air pocket of no time jam the gears so that they stop entirely. The earth comes to a stop as well, for time has been stopped. God's command stopped the sun and moon in its orbit so Joshua could win the battle. All of Israel was feared after that day, and there has not been a day like it since. We can have those days if we only ask.

I tell my soul to follow the path of stillness that leads to God's righteous wisdom, wisdom that teaches me how to live in quietness so that I may hear the voice of the Lord direct me. I find it interesting that Jesus asked the disciples, "Why are you afraid? Have you still no faith?" Jesus uses the word again, "still," along with the words "no faith." Therefore, we must have faith that both motivates action and knows when to be still. No matter what it is that is causing us to fear, we must remember, "Greater is He in me than he that is in the world."

Run, soul, run and jump into the air pocket of God's stillness. For every moment counts. Breathe, soul, the breath of God. Inhale and exhale, for He will refresh you with the strength of His quietness.

Chapter 29

God's Exam

I am standing at the edge of a canyon in Heaven, like the Grand Canyon in Arizona. I look across to the other side and see the Father standing on a tall hill. He is looking through binoculars and appears to examine the terrain around Him. I see Him turn to face my direction. With one hand holding the binoculars up to His eyes, He waves at me with the other, and I wave back.

My soul skips with joy that the Father has looked my way and has not ignored me. I want to cross the canyon to visit and talk with Him. However, today is not the day to do so. He waves goodbye to me, walks up the hill, and disappears.

I sit down on the flat edge of a large stone and look over the great vastness of the canyon. As I survey its breathtaking beauty, I sit in quietness. I see an eagle soar in the air with its wings spread out as it glides above in the sky. I think about how some people are afraid of God examining them up close, even more so when they are far from Him.

What does God see when He looks at us? It is simple; He looks at our hearts, examining closely to see if they need to be circumcised. King David wrote in a Psalm 51 about God creating a clean heart in him and renewing a right spirit within him. Over and over, God's word speaks about matters of the heart and the importance of keeping our heart clean before Him. God does not care about your outer appearance as much as He cares about your inward person concerning spiritual heart issues. The heart is where all our happy and sad moments are stored. Therefore, God wants His prodigal sons and daughters to come home to Him with true repentance from the heart, and He will lavish you with His blessings like you were never apart from Him.

When God sets His eyes on you, He sees all the good in you and only desires to give you all the good He can give, just like an earthly father with his child. We can be so much harder on ourselves because we know in our souls, we always need to have clean hearts before the Lord . Even when we fail in our walks with the Lord, the solution is still simple. Once you see the error of your way, then do what Jesus said to do: "Repent and go and sin no more." How much more clear can the word of God be?

God does not have tunnel vision or bad eyesight. In fact, when you read His word, you can find out just how healthy He is physically. Oh, by the way, His hearing is in great shape too. If we feel His mercy when we allow the Lord to examine us up close, just think how much more we will feel His mercy when we are the prodigal children coming home to Him and He is waving at us in the distance, excited to see us. And when we arrive home, He puts His best garments on us to show how much He has missed us and how glad He is that we returned home changed in our hearts.

Our Father in Heaven loves us and puts us through the heart test so we can pass the exam even while we live far off from Him. God always makes a way for those who are called according to His purpose.

God is a just judge, so it is important to know that "God chastises those He loves" (Hebrews 12:6). I know what you are thinking about right now: "Then He must love me an awful lot!"

Proverbs 22:6 says, "Teach a child in the way he should go, and when he is old, he will not depart from it." We can bring a lot of hardship on ourselves sometimes, yet somehow, we want to forget our own part in it because we are looking to place the blame on anybody but ourselves. It does not matter what sin you have committed. When you call out to the Lord with a sincere heart, He will answer, "Here I am."

Wow! How gracious our Father in Heaven is. He will move a mountain for you, part the waters, give you fire by night to provide light, and send a cloud by day to give you shade. Oh, my soul, let the Father come close to examine your heart so you can live an everlasting life in Him. He will widen His path beneath you, so you do not slip and fall.

"I will praise You, O Lord, with my whole heart; I will tell of all your marvelous works" (Psalm 9:1).

In the Lord I put my trust; how can you say to my soul, "Flee like a bird to your mountain"? ² For look! The wicked bend their bow, they make ready their arrow on the string, that they may shoot secretly at the upright in heart. ³ If the foundations are destroyed, what can the righteous do?

⁴ The Lord is in His holy temple, the Lord's throne is in Heaven; His eyes behold, His eyelids test the sons of men. ⁵ The Lord tests the righteous, but the wicked and the one who loves violence His soul hates. ⁶ Upon the wicked He will rain coals; fire and brimstone and a burning wind shall be the portion of their cup.

For the Lord is righteous, He loves righteousness; His countenance beholds the upright. (Psalm 11)

The word of the Lord is dependable to deliver the upright in heart. His words are pure, like silver tried in a furnace of earth, purified seven times. You shall keep them, O Lord; You shall preserve them from this generation forever. Lord, who may abide in Your tabernacle? Who may dwell in Your holy hill? He who walks uprightly, and works righteousness, and speaks the truth in his heart. We must do what is right continually before the Lord, so we will not be moved.

"I have called upon You, for You will hear me, O God; incline Your ear to me, and hear my speech. Show Your marvelous lovingkindness by Your right hand, O You who save those who trust in You from those who rise up against them" (Psalm 17:6-7).

As I continue to ponder on keeping my heart right before the Father, I realize that it is time to leave the beauty of the canyon. I stand up and begin to walk down a nearby path. I see a note laying on a stone with an apple on top of it, and I smile as I pick it up, for my soul knows instantly that the Father was near me the whole time. Tears come to my eyes, and I am overcome, for He was examining me up close and wanted to be near me even when I least expected it.

The note reads, "Victorious, thank you, for I was able to draw near to you because of your heart so pure before me. I will keep you as the apple of my eye; I will hide you under the shadow of My wings." I fall to my knees honoring the God of glory, who gave so unselfishly His Son Jesus so that I might have life and more abundantly. I say out loud to my Father, "Keep me as the apple of Your eye; hide me under the shadow of Your wings all the days of my life."

I stand up, holding the note dear to my heart, and take a bite of the apple He gave me. As I chew the crisp, juicy fruit, my soul says, "Truly I can taste and see how good the Lord is to me. I am blessed of the Lord, for I choose to take up my cross daily, follow Him, and keep a righteous heart before Him." Soon, the Holy Spirit and I walk the path to the next journey the Lord has for me.

Chapter 30

The Crystal Road

One Saturday afternoon, I am sitting at my study desk reading the Bible and listening to praise and worship music. The Holy Spirit inspires me to sit quietly before the Lord, and I ask the Holy Spirit to show me what righteousness looks like in Heaven.

Before I know it, I am standing on a hill under a tree, with lush green grass beneath my feet. I look down the hill and see a field of tall yellow flowers swaying in the wind. Beyond the field, I see a brilliant, shining crystal mountain. I step into the field of yellow flowers and bend down to pick one. Just as I get ready to pick the flower, I look at my outstretched hand in front of me and realize that I am a little girl again.

The flower momentarily forgotten; I look up to see Jesus standing over me. He smiles, stoops down to meet me at eye level, and hands me a flower He picked for me. I take the flower and thank

Jesus for giving it to me. I notice that I am wearing a white dress, and Jesus is also wearing a garment of white. We stand up, He takes my hand, and I am invited to walk with Him through the field of flowers toward the crystal mountain.

By the time I reach the end of the field with Jesus, I am a grown woman again. We walk out of the field and step onto a crystal road, which we follow up to the crystal mountain. This mountain has every brilliant color you can imagine radiating from its transparent crystal glass. A glass door opens as we approach the mountain, and we enter through it.

Upon entering the crystal mountain, I hear water running. God's voice echoes all through the halls, and I see the reflection of time in the glass. This is where God's righteousness goes out to all of Heaven and earth. His throne sits at the top of the crystal mountain, and the water I hear is the river of life flowing from His throne. His river of life flows all the way from the throne through the belly of man on earth. Jesus and I walk through the halls of the crystal mountain, and I see in the reflection of the glass a radiating light that shines the righteousness of God, reminding me that He is a light unto my path.

The reflection of time is everywhere, and God's word goes out continually from this place night and day. "The commandment of the Lord is pure, enlightening the eyes; the fear of the Lord is clean, enduring forever" (Psalm 19:8-9). God's throne is on the crystal mountain because He is transparent with His righteous wisdom, holding back nothing so that man can know Him. God is so wise that He knows man will try to make every excuse to continue living in sin, instead of living in righteousness.

The inside of the crystal mountain is like a high-tech computer room full of screens that tell of all the earth's events. I see the six-day war on one of the crystal screens; on another, flood waters raging on the earth. Inside the crystal mountain is such innumerable stored data about earth that I could never contain it all. Standing in the halls of this mountain, I can clearly see why God tries so hard to befriend His own creation and documents all of man's actions on earth, so that in the end man will have no excuse for not serving the Lord.

Before long, Jesus and I reach a higher level inside the mountain, where double glass doors open onto a balcony with a transparent glass floor. We walk out on it, and the views from the balcony are stunning. I look to the right and see a waterfall I have seen before. It has an enormous, beautiful white tallit draped over the crystal cliff, with the river of life flowing over it and cascading down the mountain.

I stand on this balcony and declare that I am that unborn generation that was prophesied by King David and that righteousness was declared to, so I could say that God did this. I remember reading that Smith Wigglesworth prayed that same prayer, like King David did in the book of Psalms. Standing in this place of righteousness, I know I am that generation that they both prayed for to carry that baton to other generations as well. Smith Wigglesworth was born in 1859, and 100 years later, in 1959, I was born — a full 2,866 years after King David. It is awesome to know that I am part of an unborn generation that they saw in the far future, hoped for, and prophesied about.

It is such an honor to stand inside the crystal mountain from which God's righteousness reigns; the word of God says:

> *Who may ascend into the hill of the Lord? Or who may stand in His holy place?* *He who has clean hands and a pure heart, who has not lifted up his soul to an idol, nor sworn deceitfully.* *He shall receive blessing from the Lord, and righteousness from the God of his salvation.* *This is Jacob, the generation of those who seek Him, who seek Your face.*
>
> *Lift up your heads, O you gates! And be lifted up, you everlasting doors! And the King of Glory will come in.* (*Psalm 24:3-7*)

The time has come to leave the crystal mountain. Jesus and I walk back inside, following steps that lead downward and back to the crystal door we entered. We step back outside, onto the transparent crystal road, and I remember what King David wrote: "Worship the Lord in the beauty of holiness. The voice of the Lord is over the waters; the God of glory thunders; the Lord is over many waters; the voice of the Lord is powerful; the voice of the Lord is full of majesty. The Lord sat enthroned at the Flood, and the Lord sits as King forever" (Psalm 29:2-4, 10).

The crystal road is the smooth road that leads to righteousness before the Lord. For the word of the Lord is right, and all His work is done in truth. He loves righteousness and justice; the earth is full of the goodness of the Lord. I see more clearly now why God uses crystal glass as a symbol for righteousness. He loves transparency of the heart; nothing can be hidden from Him.

As we walk down the crystal road, I wonder why I was transformed into a child in the field of flowers and then grew into an adult before embarking on the crystal road. Jesus answers me even before I speak, "Whenever you seek Kingdom secrets, you need childlike faith to bring them into existence." I smile and reply, "I understand that completely because I am simpleminded and a big kid at heart anyway." Jesus and I laugh together and walk back across the field of yellow flowers and up the hill. I hug Him goodbye until our next visit.

I look back at the crystal mountain and am thankful for the opportunity I have had to visit. I hope that one day I will be able to return and learn more about it. Rejoice, O my soul, for you have been in the presence of God's righteousness.

Chapter 31

Dancing with the Holy Spirit

I love worship time with the Holy Spirit guiding me in how to please the Lord during my quiet time before Him. I ask the Holy Spirit to please take me to Heaven to worship this night, and He does.

I see a mighty mountain in the distance, with God's beautiful shimmering rays of light playing across it. I stand in awe of this place. Before long, the Holy Spirit leads me out onto a frozen body of water, and suddenly I am worshiping the Lord with ice skates on. The music plays, and I start to worship in the most graceful figurine ice skating that is being released upon me by the Holy Spirit. I feel my soul being engulfed by the God of glory. The power of the Holy Spirit pours down on me like rain, so pure and gentle. As I worship, Jesus appears on the shore and watches me. Angels all around Him sing that He is the risen Lamb of God and the one true Messiah.

Soon, true worshipers come and join me in worship before the Lord. Each skater moves in sync as the Holy Spirit releases sparkles of glittering light down upon us. The true worshipers move in a circle around me, and the Holy Spirit descends upon us like a dove in a cloud, shining like the softness of moonlight.

I twirl on my ice skates as the Holy Spirit moves all around me. I say out loud, "Kosher, kosher is what I want to be forever before the Lord. I want my soul and spirit to be pure before the Lord always." The true worshipers and I sing out, "Hallelujah, hallelujah, bless the Lord," as we figure skate before Him. Precious is this moment before the Lord. Bless the Lord, for He is greatly to be praised.

In Heaven, you have talents and skills you normally do not possess on earth, and what you do have on earth is increased in Heaven. My soul and spirit on earth adore worship time with the Lord. I am not talented on earth with skillful singing or dance, but in Heaven there is no such thing as an untalented individual. I always look forward to my visits to Heaven because Jesus said, "The kingdom of God is within you" (Luke 17:21) and "God is Spirit, and those who worship Him must worship in spirit and truth" (John 4:24). Therefore, in my quiet time I always release my earthly flesh to the Lord and ask the Holy Spirit to comfort me along the way, so that I can learn from the fullness of His wisdom.

If we do not go where God is, how can we expect to receive all the benefits of Heaven where He has them stored up for the taking?

He gives to those who are willing to access His Kingdom secrets, which will release to us a spiritual insight that some never dare to seek or to know. Our Father in Heaven does not want us to be afraid of seeking His Kingdom secrets. In doing so, we find Him and His good pleasures.

He desires to give His Kingdom secrets to us daily. For man cannot live by bread alone, but by every word that proceeds out of the mouth of God. No matter what you are lacking spiritually, He will gladly give to the thirsty soul that is sincerely seeking Him in truth. Self must get out of the way and allow the Holy Spirit to move and reveal God's way.

Skate, soul, skate before the Lord in His good pleasure!

My time comes to an end on the ice, and I make my way through the crowd of true worshipers toward the shore. I stand and inhale the breath of the love of God in this incredibly special place of worship and hope that one day I will return here to worship again.

I thank the Holy Spirit for bringing me here, and soon I am back on earth preparing for bedtime. For tomorrow will bring a new and exciting day with the Lord again.

Chapter 32

What God Values

My soul seeks to know what God values. It is a Friday afternoon, and I am at work, up on a ladder and painting a bedroom wall. I hear the Lord speak to me that man is trying to find value in his life. When man is reckless with his life, it is because he does not remember the One who gives him value.

I begin to weep so hard while standing on the ladder that I must pause and get quiet before the Lord to finish hearing Him speak to me. I am brokenhearted because I realize I have found myself many times in that same frame of mind. So many times, I have believed the lie of the enemy that I am worthless and not valuable to anyone, including God my Creator. I say through my tears, "God, how can You stand me? I am so weak-minded at times. When will I ever quit that kind of thinking?" He tenderly replies, "When you realize how valuable you are to Me." I ask Him to forgive me for not realizing how valuable I am to Him.

The next day, Saturday, I decide to study in the Bible about what God values, and I read in Psalm 119, "Turn away my eyes from looking at worthless things, and revive me in Your way."

We are surrounded by many worthless things, which is why finding worth in your relationship with the Lord is so important. Knowing our worth in the Lord gives us unseen strength that is beyond earthly understanding. Those who trust in the Lord are like Mount Zion, which cannot be moved but abides forever. I read in Psalm 139:13-18:

> *13 For You formed my inward parts; You covered me in my mother's womb. 14 I will praise You, for I am fearfully and wonderfully made; marvelous are Your works, and that my soul knows very well. 15 My frame was not hidden from You, when I was made in secret, and skillfully wrought in the lowest parts of the earth. 16 Your eyes saw my substance, being yet unformed. And in Your book, they all were written, the days fashioned for me, when as yet there were none of them.*
>
> *17 How precious are your thoughts to me, O God! How great is the sum of them! 18 If I should count them, they would be more in number than the sand; when I wake, I am still with You.*

I would say that means we can know without a doubt that we are valuable to God!

As I continue searching for what God values in His word, I see a vision of myself as a little child skipping down a city sidewalk without a care in the world. People rush by me, going about their daily routine and not giving me a thought. I skip to the candy store and buy my favorite candy. I pop some bubble gum in my mouth and chew it well so I can blow great big bubbles with it.

I walk slowly so I can gaze in store windows. I come upon an old man dressed in ragged clothes. He looks sad and hopeless as he sits on a bucket near one of the shop windows. My soul wonders if this is a man or an angel.

I pause in front of him and ask, "Are you okay, sir?" The man replies, "Why should I be okay, when I have no value to anyone?" I then ask if he would like a piece of chewing gum or some candy. The man takes a piece of gum, sticks it in his mouth, and starts to chew it. We start to laugh together because the man all of a sudden realizes he has worth to me.

I sit with him awhile and tell him how valuable he is to God. The old man begins to cry, and I put my hand on his to comfort him. I help him up, and as we walk together, we see who can blow the largest bubbles.

We must go into all the world and share the love of God so people will know they are valuable to Him, even when they do not feel valued by the people around them. Leave no stone unturned when it comes to sharing the love of God with others. Skip, soul, skip, for you might be entertaining an angel unaware.

Chapter 33

The Wind

One morning, I am getting ready to walk out the door to go to work, having just finished praying for people on my prayer list. As I place my prayer list back on my desk, the Holy Spirit transports me to Heaven.

I am a little girl walking beside a man riding on a white horse. It is light around us, but dark in front of us. We climb a hill, and as the light around us expands, I look below and see lush rolling hills with some of the most beautiful pastures I have ever seen. The tall grass sways gently in the wind.

I sense in my soul that the Lord wants me to know that the wind that blows in Heaven is not like the wind on earth. The wind in Heaven is full of God's Spirit; it is alive and comes directly from His throne. I speak out loud, "Where my Father leads, I will go. I will not be swayed to and fro like a chime hanging on a porch hook that swings back and forth, making a lot of noise but going nowhere." He is a light unto my path, guiding me forward safely in the dark.

Now I see who is on the horse: the Heavenly Father. He has been leading me since I was a child. He watches over the orphans because He is a Father to the fatherless. My journey has brought me alongside my Heavenly Father today to remind me who has been guiding my steps on earth. I stand beside Him today as a child with great humility and declare, "He is high and lifted up in all of Heaven and earth." He wears a crown upon His head and a purple velvet cape around His shoulders, with a pure gold cord to fasten it in place.

He offers me His hand and pulls me up behind Him on the horse, where I throw my arms around Him with childlike trust. I press the right side of my face up against His back and inhale His breath, His love, His kindness, His gentleness, His protection, and every ounce of His good pleasure toward me. I begin to cry tears of joy because my Heavenly Father wants me to be with Him and participate in what He is doing in Heaven and on earth. Today, I have been invited to draw closer to Him than ever before.

Rejoice, O my soul; inhale and exhale the breath of God in this precious moment. Learn, soul, learn and never let go of God's helping hand, which lends to the poor and gives food to the needy. His quiver is full of benefits for you.

I am royalty, riding with my Father on His royal horse in His Kingdom. He takes me riding through green pastures and alongside babbling brooks in the countryside. I do not have to speak because this is a time for me to be still and know that He is God, the Creator of all things great and small. I feel so much peace within me as we ride throughout the land of Heaven.

We come to a stop, and the Father helps me off the horse. I see a woman standing under a tree and smiling at both of us. She waves to me to come to her. As I walk toward her, she invites me to sit with her on a royal blanket that is spread out over the ground. The Father dismounts his horse and comes to sit down on the blanket beside us.

As the woman hugs me, I notice how beautiful she is. She shares a look with the Father that tells me she is glad to see me. She nods her head at Him as they speak in a language I cannot understand. Then I hear her say in English, "She is ready."

She has raised my childlike curiosity, and I am anxious to understand what she means. She turns to me and says, "Victorious, you are here today because you stayed on the path of righteousness, even when it did not seem to benefit your walk in the Lord. You have shown yourself to be steadfast in your faith, and no matter how you have been made fun of by others, you have stayed the course. You have remembered that through Christ you can do all things. You have put your trust in the One whom the Father called from the beginning of man."

I listen intently, not wanting to miss a word. I nod my head to let her know that I am listening and absorbing what she is saying to me.

She touches my little cheek with her right hand and says, "You remind me a lot of myself when I lived on earth as Queen Esther. I had to face a lot of challenges and stand against wickedness to save my people from extinction. Keep pushing forward, Victorious, and you will prevail because you seek the Father's wisdom in all you do. You will help others along the way to achieve spiritual freedom and much more. Prepare this day, for you have been invited to walk the path of gold, which will lead you into a deeper relationship with the Father. A greater understanding is about to be given unto your soul like man has never seen before. Are you ready?"

"Yes," I say, "yes! I am ready." I turn to the Father and say, "I will serve you all the days of my life. I will freefall into your everlasting wisdom, knowledge, and understanding. I am free, I am free!" I shout. "He who is in Christ is a new creation indeed. Where the Spirit of the Lord is, there is liberty!"

I hug Esther goodbye and thank her for sharing the good news with me. Father mounts His horse, lends His hand to me, and lifts me back up behind Him. We wave goodbye to her and ride off. This time, I rest my left cheek on the back of my Father as I cry more tears of joy. Again, I inhale His life in me. I thank Him with every breath in my lungs, so grateful for His care for me.

He tells me to hold on as the horse breaks into a fast trot. I hold on for dear life, the wind blowing through my hair as my Father rushes me to the next path I must take. We come to a fence, which the horse leaps over, and we continue to move at a fast pace, so I do not miss my destiny, for I was born for such a time as this.

He slows the horse down as we arrive at the gold path. The Father pauses, helps me off the horse, and says, "You can make it from here, for I will be with you always, even unto the ends of the earth."

I reply, "Thank You Father. I love You and appreciate all the time You took with me today. Though I was in a hurry to go to work on earth, You wanted me to slow down so I could learn to do Your work, for my life is not my own, but Yours." He smiles and nods His head before riding off on His horse down the gold path.

As I watch Him ride off on the path ahead of me, I am comforted to know that He will already have been where He is taking me. He will make my path straight. I need not fear, for the Lord is with me. This I know for sure: that wherever He leads, I will follow. I will lean not unto my own understanding, but His.

Let the wind of Heaven blow all around me, swirling God's love through the air I breathe, bringing His Holy Spirit power upon my soul. I bow my head in humility and wait upon the Lord to show me what is next.

Chapter 34

The Gold Path

The next morning, during the week approaching the Jewish festival Rosh Hashanah, I am reclining on the couch in my living room and being quiet before the Lord. I am praying for loved ones and people I know and seeking the Lord about the gold path.

As I recline, I think about my visit to Heaven and everything Esther said to me about the greater understanding I was about to receive. "Are you ready?" I remember her asking.

In an instant, I am back on the gold path, watching the Heavenly Father ride off on His horse. I hear the Holy Spirit confirm that "the Father will have already been where he is sending you, and He will make your way straight. He will make you the head and not the tail." I begin to cry because I know I am not worthy of my Savior's love that He keeps pouring out on me each day.

I call to my Father riding away on the horse, "Father, I need You in every area of my life. I know it seems like I must go down this new path alone, but I know You will keep Your word and be with me always. Your love, wisdom, and truth will guide me and will never lead me astray." Father stops the horse, turns toward me, and waves one last time to let me know He heard me. Then He continues and disappears across the horizon.

I begin to travel down the gold path, which starts forming a transparent, softly glowing golden dome over me that moves with me with every step I take. Flaming arrows begin flying toward me, but they hit the golden dome and bounce off.

Immediately, I receive wisdom about what these arrows are. They are the fiery darts of the devil, and they cannot come through the dome that is all around me or above me. Why? Because God put His shield of protection, the dome, over me. Because it is made of pure gold, heat cannot penetrate it. I remember that the astronauts use gold in outer space to protect them from the sun's heat and see that this knowledge has been graciously given by God to man. I will bless the Lord who has given me counsel. I shall not be moved.

"Let all those rejoice who put their trust in You; Let them ever shout for joy, because You defend them; let those also who love Your name be joyful in You. For You, O Lord, will bless the righteous; with favor You will surround him as with a shield" (Psalm 5:11-12).

28 For You will light my lamp; the Lord my God will enlighten my darkness. 29 For by You I can run against a troop, by my God I can leap over a wall. 30 As for God, His

152

way is perfect; the word of the Lord is proven; He is a shield to all who trust in Him.

32 It is God who arms me with strength and makes my way perfect.

35 You have also given me the shield of your salvation; your right hand has held me up, your gentleness has made me great. 36 You enlarged my path under me. So, my feet did not slip. (Psalm 18:28-30, 32, 35-36)

I walk along the gold path, staring in awe at what is ahead of me. Though it seems far off, I know that I will soon approach it.

The Lord has anointed the righteous through Jesus the Messiah with His Spirit to bring good tidings to the poor; He has sent us to heal the brokenhearted, to proclaim liberty to the captives and the opening of prisons to those who are bound; to proclaim the acceptable year of the Lord. We who know the Lord must bring the good news of the gospel to a lost and hurting world. How will they know if we do not go and tell them that today is the day of their salvation? Today is the acceptable day of the Lord.

So many people are living without the protective shield of the Lord because they do not know how valuable they are to Him. As I walk on the gold path, I feel His care for me down to the depths of my soul. As I am wrapped all over in His love, kindness, and wisdom, I stop and fall to my knees weeping, for I long for others to know God the way I do in this very moment.

I have always read in the book of Psalms about His protective shield, and here on the gold path I find myself in the very midst of it as He shows me just how well the shield works. There is no flaw in it. It does withstand the attack of the enemy on all sides. Hallelujah, for my God reigns! Being under the shield of God's protection is what putting on the full armor of God means:

Put on the whole armor of God, that you may be able to stand against the wiles of the devil. [12] For we do not wrestle against flesh and blood, but against principalities, against powers, against the rulers of the darkness of this age, against spiritual hosts of wickedness in the Heavenly place. [13] Therefore, take up the whole armor of God that you may be able to withstand in the evil day, and having done all, to stand.

[14] Stand therefore, having girded your waist with truth, having put on the breastplate of righteousness, [15] and having shod your feet with the preparation of the gospel of peace; [16] above all, taking the shield of faith with which you will be able to quench all the fiery darts of the wicked one. [17] And take the helmet of salvation, and the sword of the Spirit, which is the word of God; [18] praying always with all prayer and supplication for all the saints - [19] and for me, that utterance may be given to me, that I may open my mouth boldly to make known the mystery of the gospel, [20] for which I am an ambassador in chains; that in it I may speak boldly, as I ought to speak. (Ephesians 6:10-20)

Though I am not in chains like Paul was in this passage of scripture, I seek the same boldness he desired. May the path I walk with the Lord help others come to know and understand just how vast God's thoughts and love toward us are. He wants to help us be strong in our walk with Him and know why we are on our specific path as we learn to live for Him. Seek, and you shall find Him. He will not hold back His goodness from you. He desires to reveal His mysteries to us.

I stand to my feet, wipe the tears from my cheeks, and look ahead — not looking to the left or right, but keeping my eyes fixed on the Lord in front of me. Soon I will meet the glorious destiny the Lord has for me on the gold path, for I can do all things through Christ who strengthens me. Fear not, O my soul, for the Lord is with you. I will wear the shield of faith, the shield of salvation, the shield of protection all the days of my life, for I am a child of the King.

Chapter 35

Walk in the Spirit

As I continue down the gold path, I see a mighty angel of God battling an unseen enemy of darkness, the one always at war with the flesh of man. All I can see is its dark silhouette, wielding a shining sword. The angel of the Lord fights fearlessly against the angel of darkness. Both angels draw their swords, and each time the shimmering weapons clash together in midair, they make a sound like a deafening thunderclap. I am scared at first, but then I remember that I am under the protection of the Lord, for I am His beloved. He watches over those who are His.

I begin to ask the Holy Spirit to let me fully understand what I am seeing. The Holy Spirit reminds me to "walk in the Spirit, and you shall not fulfill the lust of the flesh. For the flesh lusts against the Spirit and the Spirit against the flesh, and these are contrary to one another, so that you do not do the things that you want to. But if you are led by the Spirit; you are not under the law" (Galatians 5:16-18).

I am further reminded, "The fruit of the Spirit is love, joy, peace, longsuffering, kindness, goodness, faithfulness, gentleness, self-control. Against such there is no law. And those who are in Christ's have crucified the flesh with its passions and desires. If we live in the Spirit, let us also walk in the Spirit" (Galatians 5:22-25).

The Holy Spirit also brings the fourth chapter of James to mind:

4 Whoever therefore wants to be a friend of the world makes himself an enemy of God.... 6 God resists the proud but gives grace to the humble.

7 Therefore, submit to God. Resist the devil and he will flee from you. 8 Draw near to God and He will draw near to you. Do not be double-minded. 10 Humble yourselves in the sight of the Lord, and He will lift you up.

I reply to Holy Spirit, "I understand much better now how important it is to stay humble in my walk with the Lord, for the battle belongs to Him." And the Holy Spirit reminds me of other truths from God's word:

Do not be deceived, God is not mocked; for whatever a man sows, that he will also reap. 8 For he who sows to his flesh will of the flesh reap corruption, but he who sows to the Spirit will of the Spirit reap everlasting life. 9 And let us not grow weary while doing good, for in due season we shall reap if we do not lose heart. 10 Therefore, as we have opportunity, let us do good to all, especially to those who are of the household of faith. (Galatians 6:7-10)

Now thanks be to God who always leads us in triumph in Christ, and through us diffuses the fragrance of His knowledge in every place. ¹⁵ For we are to God the fragrance of Christ among those who are being saved and among those who are perishing. (2 Corinthians 2:14-15)

I move forward and leave the fierce battle behind me, for the battle belongs to the Lord; therefore, it cannot affect my walk with the Lord. His Spirit lives in me, and I trust in the One who redeems me. The transparent gold dome, my shield of protection, continues to move with me, covering me with every step I take. God's angels are with me on every side and push away any obstacle that tries to break God's barrier around me.

I see a structure of some sort in the distance, but I cannot yet make out what it is. I will keep moving forward with confidence because I know God cares for me and I am valuable to Him. He will always have my best interest at heart. King David describes it best:

I have set the Lord always before me; because He is at my right hand I shall not be moved. ⁹ Therefore, my heart is glad, and my glory rejoices; My flesh also will rest in hope. ¹⁰ For You will not leave my soul in Sheol, nor will You allow Your Holy One to see corruption. ¹¹ You will show me the path of life; in Your presence is fullness of joy; at Your right hand are pleasures forevermore. (Psalm 16:8-11)

I can rejoice and have confidence that the same resurrection power that raised Jesus from the grave will defend me. I am covered by the blood of the Lamb.

Chapter 36

The Dreams

Though my journey may take me far from my comfort zone, I will always be able to return to a place of comfort with the confidence of the Holy Spirit. For God did not leave us orphans when He resurrected Jesus from the grave.

As I wait upon the Lord to allow me to continue the path of gold, I am given two dreams.

In the first dream, I am in a room of soft pink. Women of all ages are dressed in pastel pant suits with hats to match, and I am invited to put one on as well. But for some reason, I do not feel good about being in this place. It does not bring joy to me, but fear. As I start to leave, a Black woman dressed in a pastel green pantsuit approaches me and tells me it is time for me to put a pantsuit on. She points to some doors down a hallway and tells me I can change clothes in one of those rooms. "No!" I reply as I start running toward the exit.

I run out into the foyer and through the double doors, but I realize I cannot go anywhere. I keep running through the same double doors over and over, being forced back into the room I just left. Then, suddenly, a door opens to the right of me. I bolt through the door, finally able to leave the dream, and wake up.

The next dream occurs during the week of Rosh Hashanah. At two o'clock in the morning, I am preparing to write the final sentence in the chapter "The Gold Path" when I feel a soft touch on my head. I have a feeling I will receive a dream from the Lord tonight.

I fall asleep shortly after hitting the bed, and my dream begins with me standing in the hall of a large convention center, where people gather before they go into the auditorium. I see a friend who is a missionary with other people standing around her, excited that they will be speaking to such a large audience. People are lined up, waiting for the doors to open. I am excited as well.

So, when the doors open, I enter and am surprised to see the same pink room from my previous dream. But this time, I am not afraid. As I see more and more people entering and sitting in the pews, I hear voices chatting about how excited they are that I am here and how excited they are to hear me speak. I see two men dressed in black suits, one sitting down and the other standing up like an usher. I walk to the back of the room, look around, and see an infant's white coffin in a small corner of the wall. I immediately want to get out of the pink room.

I find a door, exit the pink room, and step into a funeral home. One of my sisters, who is four years younger than me, is preparing for a funeral for several generations that have already passed away, including our dad. I see her and her mother-in-law putting up small statues of children and placing them in groups. Each child is from a different generation. As strange as this scene appears, I am still not afraid, so I continue toward the back of the funeral home. A door swings open, and one of my sisters, who is four years older than me, steps in. She hangs a blue dress on a hook that she will soon put on for the funeral. I think to myself that if my other sister is coming to the funeral, I guess everyone else in my family will come too.

When I wake up from the dream, I am perplexed about what it means. As I ponder the two dreams over and over, the Holy Spirit tells me, "Pray for all generations in your family and others, for the last enemy to be conquered through Jesus' death is death itself."

When Jesus was resurrected from the grave, He immediately conquered death. Yet the enemy still has a stronghold in my family and others when it comes to death. The enemy comes to kill, steal, and destroy. I know now that I am to pray for the unborn and children of all ages who are still alive. I pray for all the women who have been affected by the loss of a child, whether a miscarriage, an untimely death, or an abortion. I realize that the blue dress represents the tears that have been shed by women losing a child. It does not matter how old you are; losing a child of any age deeply affects the soul within you.

I stop what I am doing and pray a fervent prayer of protection over all the women in my family and others. I feel the heaviness leave my soul and weep for a while, for I know how many lives the enemy has stolen from our family throughout the generations. The enemy thinks he can win the battle against us through death, but death empowers us that much more through Christ, because death is the last enemy for Jesus to defeat. We have an everlasting life waiting for us in Heaven. But this promise does not mean we just give up; it enables us to run the race at a much smoother pace and only die when God wants us to, not when the devil wants us to.

The enemy has no power other than what we give him. Just like a real battle in a field of soldiers, the battle is won by how well the general's leaders follow the plan to win the battle and relay those instructions to their troops so fewer casualties happen.

Soldiers must be trained before they can fight in a battle so that they will know how to conquer the enemy. The same applies to believers. The Lord has said that the battle belongs to Him; therefore, He wants to teach us how to combat the unseen enemy in our lives so that we have fewer moments of failure against him.

A few days after the second dream, on a Sunday, my husband and I are driving down the highway toward home. Lined up along the sidewalks are several people holding up signs with pro-life messages on them, just beginning a rally for the unborn. I immediately remember my dreams about praying for children of all generations.

As I see all these people lining the sidewalks to take a stand for the unborn, I feel in my spirit that prayer can bring protection over our generations yet to come. I know my own prayers fought an unseen battle just a few days before, and God answered in a short time with these people who are not ashamed to take a bold stance against abortion. Praise God I found the boldness to step back into the pink room and continue beyond it so I could fully understand the message. Because I had already traveled on the path of gold and seen God's dome of protection over me, I was less afraid of the unknown territory of the pink room. I am reminded that I must keep pushing forward.

Fear not, O my soul, for the Lord is with you.

Chapter 37

On a Roller Coaster

The gold path has brought more questions than answers thus far, but I know the Lord will reveal all of them to me in due time. For God is my best friend, I am deeply in love with Him, and He is in love with me. He will help me through the challenges of the race I run. My Heavenly Father is my Wisdom and will provide all the guidance I need as I move along the path of gold.

I look around and see the wonders of Heaven all around me, a realm that is far beyond the physical world of mankind. As I move down the path, I feel His love so deep in my soul that I begin to cry, stopping in the middle of the gold path and bowing my head low. Soon, I fall to my knees, weeping and soaking in His deep unconditional love for me. He begins to soothe my soul with His presence. I feel His heartbeat within me, and I know He is all-caring and will never leave me. No matter what I must go through, I know He is with me.

"Father," I say, "My heart has been on a roller coaster with all the challenges of the world I have been dealing with the last several weeks. Being there when my mother-in-law passed away and left this earth to walk into her everlasting life with You was so overwhelming for me, even though I know she is in a much better place now. I am not sure why You chose me to be there for her when it came time for her to cross over into her new life in You, and yet I can somehow figure out why You did pick me.

"During the journey you have led me on, the Holy Spirit has taught me to have a better understanding of death and life. In the end, what matters is that we had a real relationship with You while on earth. Did we 'seek You while You may be found' during our earthly life, and if so, what did we do with that information?"

I hear a horse galloping toward me on the gold path, and soon it stops beside me. I look up and see Father seated upon it. As He reaches down to me, I stand up, lean against the horse, and start crying again, my face now buried in its beautiful mane. Father strokes my hair gently and says, "Now, come, let us go from this place, and I will journey with you while you lean on Me and not unto your own understanding."

I reach out, and He pulls me up on the back of the horse. I hold onto Him tightly as we gallop off onto the path before us. As I lean into Him and lay my right cheek on His back, I feel my tears wet His soft velvet purple cape. It is quiet as we ride along, and I hear our hearts beating in sync with each other. "Father," I whisper, "I love

You. Thank You for loving me back. Your love for me is so great. Thank you for not abandoning me. I need You, Father, and Your breath of life which is constant in me."

I hold onto Father, and we ride awhile. He stays with me a great distance. He does not let me walk but carries me many miles along the path, until I stop crying and my spirit has become quiet before Him. He reminds me to be still and know that He is God, my Abba Father, and the lover of my soul.

The horse comes to a stop, and I look in front of us and see Jesus wearing a white robe and standing on the side of the road. The Father tells Him, "I have brought Victorious to You, and she will follow You the rest of the journey on the gold path. Go in shalom." He helps me off the horse, and I smile and thank Him for His undying love for me.

I turn and walk toward Jesus. He smiles and extends His hand out to me. We begin our walk on the gold path, chatting as we go. I pause and thank Jesus for being my friend and caring enough to walk this path with me, for it has been difficult. I see the vision of God's love for us on the day He tore the curtain in the temple — when Jesus said, "It is finished," the day he died on the cross, and the dead in Christ were resurrected from the grave.

The same power that raised Jesus from the grave moves in those who are called according to His purpose. We can now come boldly before the throne of the Father with no barrier, unafraid and in perfect peace, knowing that He is there for us even in death. He unveils our sin so that His will may be done on earth as it is in Heaven. Even through trial and tribulation, we can depend on our Father in Heaven to guide us with His wisdom to a great and glorious destiny, just as He guided Jesus while He was here on this earth.

Chapter 38

The High Priest

As Jesus and I walk together along the gold path, the quietness around us soothes me. His strength quiets the innermost being of my spirit, for He is the lover of my soul.

Jesus leads me to a hill, where an angel brings Him a shofar. He lifts it to His mouth and blows it in the direction of a city with a wall around it. I see the double-arched stone doors on the wall and can tell that they have been closed for an exceptionally long season.

The sound of the shofar shakes the stones that have been used to keep the doors blocked. The stones begin to crumble down to the ground, and the doors blast open. The graves beyond shake and crack and fall open as well. Behold, judgment will now lay waiting for those who did not enter His rest but failed to enter because of their disobedience. I see Jesus step up on a cornerstone, and I know immediately what the message is, for He is the stone that the builders rejected.

We must not cast away our confidence in Jesus the High Priest, because such confidence has great reward for those who hold fast in times of trouble and longsuffering:

For you have need of endurance, so that after you have done the will of God, you may receive the promise:

37 "For yet a little while, and He who is coming will come and will not tarry. 38 Now the just shall live by faith; but if anyone draws back, My soul has no pleasure in him."

39 But we are not of those who draw back to perdition but of those who believe to the saving of the soul. (Hebrews 10:36-39)

Now faith is the substance of things hoped for, the evidence of things not seen. 2 For by it the elders obtained a good testimony.

3 By faith we understand that the worlds were framed by the word of God, so that the things which are seen were not made of things which are visible. (Hebrews 11:1-3)

I stand in awe of my Savior, of whom God Himself said:

Behold, I lay in Zion a stone for a foundation, a tried stone, a precious cornerstone, a sure foundation; whoever believes will not act hastily. 17 Also, I will make justice the measuring line, and righteousness the plummet; the hail will sweep away the refuge of lies, and the waters will overflow the hiding place. 18 Your covenant with death will be annulled, and your agreement with Sheol will not stand. (Isaiah 28:16-18a)

¹ Woe to the crown of pride, to the drunkards of Ephraim, whose glorious beauty is a fading flower…. ⁵ In that day the Lord of hosts will be for a crown of glory and a diadem of beauty to the remnant of His people, ⁶ for a spirit of justice to him who sits in judgment, and for the strength to those who turn back the battle at the gate. (Isaiah 28:1, 5-6)

¹⁹ Open to me the gates of righteousness; I will go through them, and I will praise the Lord. ²⁰ This is the gate of the Lord, through which the righteous shall enter.

²¹ I will praise You, for you have answered me, and have become my salvation.

²² The stone which the builders rejected has become the chief cornerstone. ²³ This was the Lord's doing; it is marvelous in our eyes. ²⁴ This is the day the Lord has made; we will rejoice and be glad in it. (Psalm 118:19-24)

Oh, give thanks to the Lord, for He is good! For His mercy endures forever. (Psalm 136:1)

The veil must be removed from our hearts so we can clearly see who Jesus is and why He was appointed the High Priest and Chief Cornerstone by God the Father. I am grateful that Jesus has chosen to take me down this path so I can bear witness to who He is. I am grateful that He has shown me the importance of sharing His love with others so they too can bear witness of Him.

The trumpet is about to be blown. May the Lord remove all hardness from our hearts so we can receive salvation and enter into His rest, worshiping Him together on His holy mountain in Jerusalem.

Chapter 39

Watchers

As Jesus and I continue traveling down the gold path, we talk about the doors of the city that blasted open. He reminds me of the vision He showed me during a prayer time recently of the walls of Jerusalem on fire. It was not a fire that burns physically; it was a fire that was connected to the Holy Spirit, the One who penetrates the hearts of men.

The Lord spoke to me on the day of the vision and said, "I am calling watchers to pray over My chosen city Jerusalem. Jerusalem is Mine, and I watch over it day and night. I seek watchers to pray for Jerusalem so that My Ruach will be released like a fire upon My people Israel, so that they too will be redeemed at My coming." I saw myself back at the Wailing Wall praying for the shalom of Jerusalem when I went there in 2016.

It is not the multitude of your words that the Lord seeks in your prayer time with Him; it is the sincerity of your heart before Him that gets His attention. Until we realize we are utterly lost without Him, we can never move His Holy Spirit fire to reach our hearts or the hearts of others.

Jesus, You mean the world to me. Thank You for showing me the way that I should go, for You truly are the Way, the Truth, and the Life. You have given the world hope. You are my hope, and I will continue to stand in the gap for Jerusalem, asking for Your Holy Spirit fire to be released upon all of Jerusalem.

A few days after the Lord had given me the vision of the walls of Jerusalem on fire, I met a woman at a conference who told me she was putting together a prayer group to pray especially for Jerusalem. I told her she was an answer to my prayer and told her of the vision I had, and she was so excited to know that the Lord was calling others to stand in the gap for Jerusalem in these last days. God will save Jerusalem, so that her salvation will come forth for the world to see.

Jesus and I continue our walk along the path of gold, and soon we reach a city with stone walls. He enters the city with me, and as we walk on her streets of stone, I can see how much He loves every inch of this place.

We pause for a moment on the street, and I see now where we are. We are in Jerusalem, the city of our Father. My eyes fill with tears of joy as I hear the Holy Spirit say, "Dance in her streets to the Lord!" Jesus and I laugh together, and I begin to dance.

A small, flowing banning appears in my hand. I twirl it as I dance to the sound of the music that the angels play. I worship in spirit and truth before the Lord in the city of my God, dancing just like David danced. In Heaven, in this holy city, I can dance for many hours in the streets without getting tired. The Holy Spirit gives me free rein to move about the city streets without disturbance.

God is calling His remnant back to Israel, and He is ready to give redemption. Though He scattered them among the nations, He says He will be a sanctuary for them no matter what country they are living in when He calls them. He will remove their hearts of stone, and they will return to him.

Seek, my soul, seek the Father so you can be redeemed forever in His grace and mercy.

Chapter 40

Beauty for Ashes

As I stand on the stone street in Jerusalem with Jesus, an elderly woman clothed in rags comes and sits on a small stone wall near us and begins to play beautiful violin music. The woman starts to cry as she plays the violin, and I soon find myself engulfed by the Holy Spirit as I begin to dance and sing in front of her. I sing a song inspired by Zephaniah 3:

"O daughter of Zion do not be sad. It will not be long, and your Father will come for you and will bring your groom who will take away all your iniquities and redeem you. You will trade in your rags, and He will replace them with beautiful linen fit for royalty. And on that day, His word says, He will restore to the people a pure language, that they all may call on the name of the Lord, to serve Him with one accord, and no one shall make them afraid ever again.

"You will sing, O daughter of Zion! And will Shout, O Israel. Shout, O Israel! You will be glad and rejoice with all your heart, O daughter of Jerusalem! The Lord has taken away your judgments; He has cast out your enemy. The king of Israel, the Lord is in your midst; You shall see disaster no more."

The music stops, and the woman fades away. I turn to look at Jesus, who tells me that I will soon be leaving Jerusalem. The same creature that flew me to the castle and forest will take me to a new place so that I can continue my journey running the good race of righteousness. I thank Jesus for spending time with me and hug Him.

Soon, the creature swoops in, lands on the stone street, and kneels so I can climb on. I wave to Jesus and tell Him I love Him greatly, and the creature takes off flying with me on his back. I feel a joy I cannot contain. I am grateful for all that the Lord has shown me while on this journey of seeking to know Him better and growing closer to Him than I have ever been before. For it is true that the kingdom of Heaven always lives in me and all around me . No matter where I am in the physical on earth, I can at any time step into Heaven's realm and gain wisdom, knowledge, and understanding for my life.

I fly for a while on the creature's back; we are not in a hurry to reach my next destination, for the Lord knows I need this quiet time to be refreshed and gain strength to continue the race. I can feel the simultaneous strength and gentleness of the Lord in creating this magnificent creature that I am riding on. I feel grateful for this moment because I know few people will have the opportunity to see such a creature in God's kingdom while living on earth.

Dusk is approaching, and the creature soon lands. I slide off his back and thank him for flying me to this new location.

I soon find myself standing on a busy street behind a car at a red light, with several cars behind me. We are all in a right turn lane, waiting for the light to turn green. I decide that since I am not in a vehicle, I will go around the car in front of me and walk to the corner.

As I move to do so, the woman in the car that's first in line to turn rolls her window down and yells that it's illegal for me to cut out of line to turn right before the light turns green. Her words seem very strange to me, since I am on foot.

Then I notice there are no cars in the lane going straight; they all seem to be turning right because that is the shortest route to home. So, I run in front of her car to get in the lane going straight. The lady yells, "That's better. Now you're doing it right!"

At first, I am the only one in line, but then a young woman comes and stands beside me and says, "I have decided to go straight too, instead of turning with everyone else." I reply, "Okay, let's do it!"

Across the intersection from us, also stopped at the red light, I see a CTS Cadillac with its headlights on. The woman driving it is going straight, like us, but in the opposite direction. In fact, I see many cars lined up to go in the opposite direction that I am going. The young lady and I stand alone.

The red light finally turns green and I call to the young woman beside me, "Let's go! The light is green, and we must hurry." We both take off running across the intersection. All the other lights stay red; no one else can go except for us.

The Lord gave me the dream about the red light twice in a row. I shared the dream with a friend who gave me great insight.

He saw the young lady who stood beside me at the red light as me when I was a young lady of 22, which is the age I accepted the Lord into my heart. I am flexible and have leadership quality, and now I must take the past with me and move forward with its wisdom.

The elderly lady wearing rags represents God taking our ashes and turning them into beauty, a beauty that surpasses all our sorrows and failures, representing a forgiveness that only a true Father can give to His child when he needs it.

Cry, soul; laugh, spirit; live in unity in the Lord, and you will be set free to accomplish your Father's will with a great and mighty love that only He can give all His creation, great and small.

Father, I look forward to a new season of adventures with You so I can keep learning about Your love for all mankind. You are gracious, wonderful, and mighty. I do not know where this new path will lead as of yet, but this one thing I know: my spirit and soul are eager to follow You wherever the new path leads.

I must take the new and the old with me on this journey. We cannot leave the past completely behind; instead, we must learn from it and run the race with its wisdom, not leaning unto our own understanding, but the Lord's.

Description

Grace to Run the Race is composed of 40 short stories that tell of God's grace to help us live victoriously through living from Heaven onto the earth. God wants to reveal His Kingdom secrets to those who ask, seek, and knock and Holy Spirit works to reveal God's wisdom about this narrow path and gives comfort while we run the race to complete our glorious destiny.

God wants us to use the realms of Heaven to our advantage so we can advance in His righteousness with success. By doing so, we can learn to experience Heaven today with the risen power of Jesus behind it all. Valerie embarks upon a journey through Heaven to solve every day real time issues and along the way she has encountered angels, living creatures, multiple gardens, a beautiful forest with all kinds of wildlife, and much more.

She has visited the corridors of Heaven and most importantly has seen first-hand how the grace and loving kindness of our Creator takes great care for all His creation, great and small. He is eager to have a relationship with us.

Valerie's story is not for the faint of heart but for the true seeker who desires a sincere relationship with Jesus which will unlock God's Kingdom secrets to win the race.

About the Author

Valerie Henderson is a native Texan, author, and guest speaker. In 2010 she published her first book under the name Val Henderson, which tells the true story of her father murdering her mother before committing suicide and how she came to forgive him. Valerie shares the story through her ministry called "Roadblock Ministry" established in 2000. She has told her story in a variety of venues across the central United States.

She is a children's artist and produced a coloring book in 2008 called *The Read Me Coloring Book*. Valerie and her husband John own a small business and have been married for over 40 years and have two children and five grandchildren. She is the 11th of 14 children.

Valerie likes keeping it real when talking about the Lord; she will not hold back to share the power of God with others. In 2006, Valerie had heart surgery just as the Lord told her she would in 1994. During the surgery, Valerie visited heaven for six hours and when she awoke, she could still see on the other side while lying in ICU. From that day forward she became a true seeker of Heaven's realms. Her childlike faith truly desires all the good pleasures of our Heavenly Father and desires for others to know Jesus as their savior and find the peace in their life which surpasses all understanding.

www.ingramcontent.com/pod-product-compliance
Lightning Source LLC
Chambersburg PA
CBHW021227090426
42740CB00006B/425